D1357060

The World's
GREATEST
GHOSTS

The World's
GREATEST
GHOSTS

Nigel Blundell
Roger Boar

Acknowledgements

For contributions, criticism and constructive advice, the authors would like to thank Rob Robbins, Margaret Nicholas, Derek Prigent, Terry Hasler, Geri Winsor, Don Mackay, Robin Corry, David Williams, Tony Harris, Dorieth Clarke and Jitka Markova.

The publishers wish to thank the following individuals and organizations for their kind permission to reproduce the photographs in this book: BBC Hulton Picture Library 51, 55; Janet and Colin Bord 136, 143; The Cinema Book Shop 171; Robert Estall 75, 137; Mary Evans Picture Library 7; Fortean Picture Library 81; National Film Archive/Stills Library 33; Peter Newark's Historical Pictures 46, 53, 149, Peter Newark's Western Americana 21, 155, 167, 172; Psychic News 45, 161, 186; Syndication International Ltd 41, 48, 181; John Topham Picture Library 59, 65, 118, 158, 191

First published in 1983 by
Octopus Books Limited
59 Grosvenor Street
London W1
Reprinted 1983

ISBN 0 7064 1771 2

Printed in Czechoslovakia
50 467/2

Contents

Introduction

"From ghoulies and ghosties and long-legetty beasties and things that go bump in the night, Good Lord, deliver us."
(*traditional Cornish prayer.*)

Many level-headed witnesses claim to have seen ghosts. Can they all have been imagining things? Hardly.

So what did they see? What are the forces behind such apparitions? Are they visitations from beyond the grave? Are they proof of an extra, unknown dimension? Or are they simply tricks of the mind?

In this crowded volume, hundreds of hauntings and other mysterious happenings are presented in a factual, unfanciful manner which is unusual among books on this subject.

The authors have delved into mysteries as familiar as the ghost ship Flying Dutchman and as unusual as the young man whose best friend was 300 years old. And there are traditional tales of terror – from the lady who travels headless in a phantom coach to the giant black dog feared as a harbinger of death.

The Flying Dutchman

Chapter
One

Vengeful Ghosts and Curses

Throughout history, man has governed his life according to certain laws and principles, a consensus natural order evolved over the centuries. Those caught defying that order face the consequences of human justice. Sometimes, though, justice is not seen to be done. Criminals go unpunished. Murders remain unsolved. But do the undetected guilty parties really get away with it? Or do eerie, inexplicable forces intervene to restore the balance in matters of life ... and death.

The bloodstone ring
Severed hand trapped a killer

Gale force winds lashed the tiny English village of Willisham, ripping slates from the roofs and tearing limbs from trees. A huge old oak shuddered before the onslaught and then, caught by one mighty gust, toppled, its roots tearing at the earth beneath.

Villagers who rushed to the spot to see if anyone was hurt stopped in horror as they gazed between the gnarled roots. There lay some human remains.

Police Constable Klug, the only bobby in the East Anglian community, was called and he ordered that the body be taken from its strange grave. One of the dismembered hands had a ring on one finger. Acting on a hunch, the grim-faced constable carried the hand to Ellen Grey, sister of a girl who had vanished mysteriously 18 years before, in 1873. Ellen screamed and then hugged the ghastly relic to her breast.

"It's Mary's," she sobbed. "The bloodstone ring was my wedding gift. She was born in March, and it was her birthstone."

Klug understood. Though the case was before his time, it was so well known in the area it had been the subject of a popular ballad.

On her 18th birthday, Mary Grey had married Basil Osborne. She had written a letter to John Bodneys, her sweetheart since childhood, asking for his forgiveness.

An hour before the groom was to take her away on the honeymoon, Mary told her sister she wanted to spend a little time alone in the upstairs room they had shared. When Osborne arrived with the carriage, she still hadn't come down. Frightened, they forced their way into the locked bedroom, but found no trace of the bride.

One window opened onto a balcony where a flight of steps led to an enclosed garden. But the garden, too, was empty.

The abandoned bridegroom died a month later. The villagers blamed a broken heart.

Now, 18 years later, the village knew what had become of Mary – for the skeleton had a broken neck! Ellen refused to give up her murdered sister's hand. It had been brought to her for a purpose, she said. That purpose must be fulfilled.

Dying, she left a bizarre provision in her will. Her housekeeper Maggie Williams was to have her estate, but must display the hand in some public place "where it may some day confront the murderer."

Maggie opened what became the finest pub in Willisham and gave the hand a place of honour on one wall. Enclosed in glass against a black velvet background, the bony ringed fingers claimed the attention of everyone.

After the shock of the exhibit had worn away, the tale of Mary's murder was a frequent topic of conversation. On a dismal March night in 1895, a stranger sat listening to scraps of the talk.

"Must have been just such a night as this that the wind ripped out that old oak tree," said the publican.

The stranger, a brooding man with a ravaged face, looked up from his glass. "I don't understand. What oak tree?" he asked.

"Have a look at the case on the wall and then we'll tell you the story," the barman told him.

Moments later, the stranger was screaming. He sagged against the wall, blood dripping from his fingers. An older man at the bar recognised him as Mary's missing former sweetheart John Bodneys.

When Constable Klug arrived, the bleeding man confessed to the murder of Mary Grey. In a frenzy of jealousy, he had found the bride alone in her room. Muffling her cries, he carried her from the house.

Bodneys insisted that he had not meant to kill her. But when they reached the big oak tree, she was struggling so hard he had broken her neck.

He left her in a shallow grave under the oak and tried to put Willisham behind him forever. But there had never been a moment of peace since the crime, and inevitably he had been compelled to return.

Committed to the local jail to await trial, he died "of no known disease" before his trial could be held. The authorities dismissed the old wives' tale that a murderer's hands sometimes drip blood when he faces the proof of his crime. But the people of the village knew what they had seen.

They buried Mary Grey's hand with the rest of her skeleton – and then ceremoniously burned the shirt smeared by John Bodneys' bloody fingers the day he came face to face with his guilt.

Bewildered butchers

Butchers at Britain's best-known meat market, London's Smithfield, complained in 1654 about weekly visits by a phantom mischief-maker. They said the ghost of a lawyer called Mallett glided between their stalls each Saturday evening, pulling joints of meat from the slabs. Traders who had hit out at him with cleavers and carving knives had merely sliced through thin air.

The fiend in bandages
"Cannibal" victim had his revenge

Only four men escaped when the British square-rigged yacht *Pierrot* capsized in the Atlantic in July 1884. Huddled in a battered dinghy, they drifted for 25 days. Near death from starvation and exposure, Captain Edwin Rutt then made a last desperate suggestion.

Lots should be drawn to determine which of the four would be eaten.

Two of the sailors agreed with Rutt, but 18-year-old Dick Tomlin, the youngest crewman, protested that he would rather die than eat human flesh.

Tomlin's resistance sealed his fate. At the first opportunity Rutt crept toward the sleeping boy and drove a knife into his neck.

The mate Josh Dudley and seaman Will Hoon had no reservations about cannibalism. When they were rescued by the yacht *Gellert* four days later, it was the slain boy's flesh that had sustained them.

The horror-stricken master of the *Gellert* rejected the idea of burial at sea. Hidden away underneath a tarpaulin, the body of the victim accompanied the three survivors to the Cornish port of Falmouth.

All three were tried and condemned to death for murder on the high seas. But the Home Secretary decided that there had been horror enough and commuted the sentence to six months' imprisonment.

No one could have known that the horrors were only beginning.

When the three men were freed from jail, they found little future. To keep body and soul together, Josh Dudley found work as a drayman. Two weeks later his team of horses saw something that frightened them in the middle of a foggy London street. Bolting, they tossed Dudley to the cobblestones where his head shattered.

Witnesses said the thing in the fog had been a figure swathed from head to foot in bloodstained bandages. After Dudley's death, the figure mysteriously vanished.

With fear beginning to take root, Captain Rutt went to the Soho slums and sought out Will Hoon. He found the old seaman far gone in drink, a sodden derelict in desperately bad health.

Rutt told Hoon that some vengeance-crazed relative was masquerading as Dick Tomlin's ghost, and he urged Hoon to help him ferret out the plotter. But Hoon wanted only more gin, and in a last delirium, he was taken to the charity ward of a hospital where he died in a screaming fit.

Witnesses said later that another patient "dressed all in bandages" had been holding Hoon down, apparently trying to soothe him. Then the patient vanished.

Now in a state of abject terror, Rutt went to the police. They scoffed at his tales of a "figure in bandages". But in view of the captain's mental condition, they offered him one night of lodging in a cell.

Rutt went gratefully to the cell, checking twice to be sure he was locked in. It was a cell block for the disturbed of London, and screams in the night were not uncommon.

But when at 3 am the police heard the captain, some distinctive quality in his cries brought warders running. They unlocked the door and went to his bunk, where Rutt lay with his knees scissored upward and his dead eyes like marbles.

Clenched in his fingers the shocked bobbies saw shreds of cotton. And bloodstained gauze.

Noose for a strangler

George Gaffney was a petty thief. He operated from London's seedy Soho red light district in the early years of this century. His crimes were all minor, except for one – and that was the most serious of all.

On the first day of March 1910, Gaffney saw on a street-seller's cart a strange three-foot length of woven silk rope which he recognised as a "thuggee cord", used by the Hindu assassins' sect in the Middle East to dispatch their victims.

Gaffney bought it. Two weeks later, he used it . . .

The cheap thief had been having problems with a girl named Bessie Graves, who expected him to marry her because she was pregnant. But Gaffney had wooed her under the alias of Arthur Eames. Now he had found a much more promising opportunity – an elderly rich widow, named Stella Fortney.

Called by an hysterical landlady, Scotland Yard detectives found Bessie Graves with the strangler's cord drawn so tightly around her throat it was embedded in the flesh. Their only clue was that the probable strangler was a man who called himself Arthur Eames.

It was little for the Yard to go on, and three weeks later Gaffney was still at large pursuing his romance with the widow.

It occurred to him one night that he would make a more impressive appearance if he called on the lady in a hansom cab. A second later he was screaming. In the half-light of the closed vehicle, George found Bessie Graves sharing the seat with him. The dead girl's eyes stared glassily into his, and the swollen tongue lolled from her mouth.

For more than a week Gaffney drank steadily, then he went to see Stella. She was far from friendly that evening, but melted when Gaffney gave her a stolen diamond ring. They shared a bottle of champagne, after which she sent him to the cellar for another. Bearing a kerosene lamp, Gaffney was halfway down the steps when Bessie Graves climbed out of the darkness to meet him.

She had succeeded in loosening the strangler's cord, which swung from her throat like a necklace. But the staring eyes were worse. Screaming Gaffney threw the lamp at her and crashed headlong to the bottom of the stairs.

Gaffney spent three weeks in hospital. And when he left he decided that he had only one chance of throwing off the ghost who would not leave him alone. If he put England behind him forever, perhaps Bessie Graves would remain there, too. He booked passage on the liner *Montrose*, for Quebec.

With renewed hope he checked into a small hotel on the eve of the voyage. In the semi-gloom of the room, he saw Bessie again.

This time she had freed herself from the silken noose and was holding it out to him. Feebly, he took it from her clawlike fingers. When he lifted his eyes again, Bessie had vanished. But the message was obvious. Gaffney sat down and began to scrawl his confession.

He told in detail of Bessie's murder and of her successive visits from the tomb. And now, he said, there was no possible escape.

Called by hotel staff, men from the Yard broke into Gaffney's room. They found the thief hanging from a beam. They read his confession and agreed at once that the case of the Soho strangler was closed.

Yet there was one element of the case that puzzled them. For the first time, a vital piece of evidence had vanished from the Yard's thief-proof vaults. It was the thuggee cord – the same cord that Gaffney used to hang himself in the closet.

Potatogeist!

A potato crisp firm called in an exorcist after a floating, headless figure terrified night-shift workers at the company warehouse in Leicester, England.

Murder on the menu
How Lazio cooked up a lethal plot

Innkeeper Lazio Kronberg and his wife Susi faced a bleak feature in the little Hungarian town of Tisakurt. It was 1919 and the couple had spent their savings trying to keep the inn going throughout the Great War. Now they had hardly enough to buy food.

There were other tragedies. Their only daughter had run away to Budapest, where she was said to be a prostitute. Their eldest son Nicholas had also run away, fleeing the house at the age of nine after Lazio whipped him for failing at school. Their other two sons had died in the war.

Night after night the old couple would sit and discuss the hopeless years ahead. At last they came to the grim decision that there was only one hope – murder for profit.

Carefully, they prepared for the killings. Lazio dug a long trench six feet deep in the woods. He filled it with quicklime, prepared to tell anyone who asked that he was planning to build new out-houses. From the village store, Susi brought home a small brown sack filled with strychnine crystals. She told the storekeeper they were going to use it to poison wolves.

Between 1919 and 1912, ten people breathed their last in the Kronberg inn. In all cases, there had been good wine with dinner and an even more remarkable vintage afterwards ... heavily laced with strychnine. The couple grew more cautious as their stolen wealth increased. There must be only one more victim, and then the quicklime pit would be sealed forever.

He came on August 14, 1922; a genial fat man in his mid-thirties, with a suitcase so heavy that it must surely contain gold coins. He had been a salesman for years, and was now looking for good land in which to invest his money.

When Susi cooked the evening meal and Lazio served it, the visitor insisted that they must be his guests for supper. And they must call him by his nickname Lucky.

Throughout the festive two-hour meal, the guest talked about his travels and was so friendly that the Kronbergs were reluctant to kill him. But it had to be done, and at last Susi brought in the "special" wine.

Their fat guest died as he drained his glass, convulsing his lips curled back from his teeth in the final spasm of strychnine poisoning.

In Lucky's bedroom, they searched his bag and saw at once they had been right. There was a fortune in gold coins. His hands shaking, Lazio pawed through the dead man's clothes and then saw something else – a snapshot of the Kronbergs themselves!

The couple looked at each other with dawning horror and grief. They had murdered their long-lost son. They left the gold and went back to the dining-room, where Nicholas was slouched at the table. They wrote a short confession and then sat down with him.

Three days later, the villagers found them, all dead from strychnine poisoning.

During the years that followed, few ventured inside the house. Those daring to stay two or three nights with a view to buying the place were always frightened off by the same grisly apparition: the sight of 13 ghostly figures from the 1920s, seated around the dining table. Each had its lips peeled back in a ghastly strychnine grin.

Another world war came and went, the house became dilapidated, but still no one would spend a night inside or even near it. Then on September 23, 1980, flames licking at the evening sky told the village that an arsonist had been at work. The old inn was reduced to ashes. No one tried to find the culprit. No one cared.

Tisakurt was at last free of its house of horror.

Murder, by a dead woman

Courtroom curse of the vengeful midget

Police have never solved one of the most bizarre murders in criminal history – for the killer was a dead woman. The roots of the crime go back to the 1870s, when Miss Ada Danforth and her little ward, Fanchon Moncare, regularly cruised between France and New York.

Miss Danforth explained that Fanchon was an orphan whose parents had died in a fire. On her 18th birthday she would inherit a fortune, but meanwhile Ada was her legal guardian.

Fanchon would curtsy adorably to any inquiring passenger and skip away with her doll. But back in their stateroom, the child masquerade ended. Fanchon's cherubic face would twist into a mask of evil. She would flay her "guardian" with the gutter language acquired from 43 years of hard living ... from her early days as a circus midget to her present career as a thief and smuggler.

In spite of the quarrels, the partnership was successful. While Ada attended to the baggage, little Fanchon – whose real name was Estelle Ridley – would dance through customs barriers still cradling her cherished doll. And no one ever dreamed of stopping her.

Afterwards, the pair would take a cab to New York's Chinatown, where Wing To, an elderly friend, waited to receive them. In the back room, the head of the doll was unscrewed and a fortune in gems spilled out – the harvest of several months' larceny on the Continent.

The business might have gone on for years but for one thing – Fanchon entered into a deadly feud with a beautiful rival, Magda Hamilton. According to police records, both women were vying for the affections of Dartney Crawley, a high stakes gambler.

Magda violated all the underworld taboos by going to the police as an informer, and the partners in crime found a reception committee waiting for them when they next docked in New York. For the first time ever, little Fanchon's doll was inspected, and minutes later the pair were en route to the notorious Tombs prison.

The midget, who had an impressive criminal record, was sentenced to life imprisonment. Ada, 10 years younger, was jailed as an accessory for 20 years.

It was Fanchon who provided the most dramatic moment of the trial. When she saw the gloating Magda sitting in the packed courtroom the midget sprang to her feet and made a shrill vow that she would one day kill her betrayer.

Triumphantly, Magda married Dartney Crawley. He deserted her six months later to try his luck in a California mining venture. But the divorce settlement was generous, and Magda was very comfortably off. Her prosperity grew through shrewd investments, and she became a prominent figure in New York café society.

Fanchon was all but forgotten by everyone ... but Magda Hamilton. One morning she burst into police headquarters and viciously cursed the officers for not letting her know that Fanchon had escaped.

She had awakened from a heavy sleep, she said, to find the midget in her bedroom. Fanchon still wore her childish finery and clutched a big china doll. But she was now a bent and withered hag, grinning with toothless gums.

Magda screamed and fled into the bathroom where she locked the door and cowered for the rest of the night.

The hysterical Magda now insisted on adequate police protection until the little monster was recaptured.

A bemused police sergeant produced a week-old copy of the *New York Sun*.

He pointed to a short item on the back page reporting that Fanchon Moncare had hanged herself in her cell.

That afternoon, Magda Hamilton booked passage for Europe on a Cunard liner. Since the ship was to leave the next day, she had a farewell dinner with a friend and then went home.

Next day the servants found her trunks neatly packed. But there would be no ocean voyage for Magda. The woman was sprawled half-naked on the bed, her eyes protruded and there was congealed blood at the corners of her mouth. According to the medical examiner, she literally drowned in her own blood. The membrane of her throat was ruptured as if some heavy object had been rammed into it with savage force.

The murder weapon was never found. But there was a clue of sorts. Lodged in Magda's bloody mouth were several hairs – similar to those found on the head of a child's china doll.

The mummy's hand

Count Louis Hamon was famed as an occultist and psychic healer. He was often given exotic presents by grateful clients he had cured. But the oddest gift of all brought him nothing but trouble.

On a visit to Luxor in 1890, Hamon cured a prominent sheik of malaria. The sheik insisted that the healer accept a gruesome gift, the mummified right hand of a long-dead Egyptian princess.

Count Hamon's wife disliked the dry, shrivelled hand from the first. But her dislike turned to horror and revulsion when she heard the story behind it. In the seventeenth and last year of his reign, King Akhnaton of Egypt – the heretical father-in-law of Tutankhamen – quarrelled over religious matters with his daughter. And the king's vengeance was ghastly.

In 1357BC, he had the girl raped and murdered by his priests. Afterwards they cut off her right hand and buried it secretly in the Valley of the Kings. The people of Egypt were appalled, for the girl would be barred from paradise because her body was not intact at burial.

Hamon would have turned the relic over to a museum, but could not find a curator willing to accept it. He locked it away in an empty safe in the wall of his London home.

In October 1922, he and his wife reopened the safe – and stood back in horror. The murdered girl's hand had changed. Shrivelled and mummified for 3,200 years, it had begun to soften with new flesh. The Countess screamed that it must be destroyed. Although he had never before been afraid of the unknown, Hamon agreed with her.

He insisted on only one thing; that the hand of the princess must have the best funeral they could give it. They were ready on the night of October 31, 1922. Halloween.

In a letter to his life-long friend, the archaeologist Lord Carnarvon, Hamon wrote that he laid the hand gently in the fireplace and read aloud a passage from the Egyptian Book of the Dead. As he closed the book there was a blast of thunder that rocked the house into total darkness. The door flew open with a sudden wind.

Hamon and his wife fell to the floor and lay there in the sudden glacial cold. Lifting their eyes, they saw the figure of a woman. In Hamon's account, "she wore the royal apparel of old Egypt, with the serpent of the House of Pharaohs glittering on her tall headdress". The woman's right arm ended in a raw stump.

The apparition bent over the fire and then was gone as suddenly as it had appeared. The severed hand had vanished with it, and was never seen again.

Four days later, Hamon read that the Carnarvon expedition had discovered Tutankhamen's tomb and that they would enter it in spite of the ancient warning emblazoned at the threshold.

From the room in the hospital where he and his wife were under treatment for severe shock, Hamon sent his old friend a letter begging him to reconsider.

He wrote, "I know now the ancient Egyptians had knowledge and power of which today we have no comprehension. In the name of God, I beg you to take care."

Carnarvon ignored the letter and soon afterwards he was dead from an infected mosquito bite. One by one, members of the expedition followed him to the grave in what became known as the Curse of the Pharaohs.

Double exorcism

Two churches were in dispute – over who had the right to exorcise the ghost of a nun. The ghost, seen first by two workmen building a multi-storey car park at Guildford, southern England, was reputed to be the spirit of a nun murdered at the spot – once a chalk quarry – hundreds of years ago.

The curate of the local Roman Catholic Church told worshippers: "I think the murdered nun was a Catholic. A Catholic priest should perform the rite".

But the local Anglican Church claimed the nun was protestant and that an Anglican should perform the exorcism. In the end they both did.

Princess of death

Egyptologist Douglas Murray neither liked nor trusted the dishevelled American who sought him out in Cairo in 1910. The man had a furtive manner and appeared to be in the final stages of disease. But Murray, a refined Briton, could not resist the blandishments of his disreputable visitor – for the American was offering him the most priceless find of his career.

It was the mummy-case of a high princess in the temple of Ammon-Ra, who was supposed to have lived in Thebes in 1600BC. The outside of the case bore the image of the princess, exquisitely worked in enamel and gold. The case was in an excellent state of preservation.

An avid collector, Murray couldn't resist. He drew a cheque on the Bank of England and took immediate steps to have the mummy-case shipped to his London home. The cheque was never cashed. The American died that evening. Murray learned from another Egyptologist in Cairo why the price had been so reasonable.

The princess from Ammon-Ra had held high office in the powerful Cult of the Dead, which had turned the fertile Valley of the Nile into a place only of death. Inscribed on the walls of her death chamber she had left a legacy of misfortune and terror for anybody who despoiled her resting place.

Murray scoffed at the superstition until three days later. That was when he went on a shooting expedition up the Nile and the gun he was carrying exploded mysteriously in his hand. After weeks of agony in hospital, his arm had to be amputated above the elbow.

On the return voyage to England, two of Murray's friends died "from unknown causes". Two Egyptian servants who had handled the mummy-case also died within a year.

Back in London, Murray found that the mummy-case had arrived. When he looked at it, the carved face of the princess "seemed to come alive with a stare that chilled the blood".

Although he had made up his mind to get rid of it, a woman friend convinced him that he should give it to her. Within weeks, the woman's mother died, her lover deserted her, and she was stricken with an undiagnosed "wasting disease". When she instructed her lawyer to make her will, he insisted on returning the mummy-case to Douglas Murray.

By now a broken wreck of a man, Murray wanted no part of it. He presented it to the British Museum, but even in that cold and scientific institution, the mummy-case was to become notorious. A photographer who

---

Racing driver's spirit

Vincent Herman was the first man to die in a crash at the old Brooklands race track, near Weybridge, Surrey. Locals say the motoring pioneer still haunts the Railway Straight where his car overturned in September 1907.

---

took pictures of it immediately dropped dead. An Egyptologist in charge of the exhibit was also found dead in his bed.

Disturbed by the newspaper stories, the board of the museum met in secret. There was a unanimous vote to ship the mummy-case to a New York museum, which had agreed to accept the gift provided it was handled without publicity and sent by the safest possible means.

The case must be shipped by the prestigious new vessel making her maiden voyage from Southampton to New York that month. All arrangements were successfully completed. But the mummy-case never reached New York. It was in the cargo hold of the "unsinkable" *Titanic* when she carried 1,498 people to their doom on April 15, 1912.

The Titanic Disaster, April 1912. The liner goes down after striking an iceberg.

A steer called "Murder"

The old West had its share of ghost stories, but none is stranger than the tale of the steer branded "Murder". From 1890 to 1920, cowhands shuddered over the legend.

The story began in 1890 in Brewster County, Texas, where the brothers Zack and Gil Spencer were rounding up longhorn cattle. The two had always been close, but tempers frayed in the hectic roundup. Suddenly there was a dispute between them over a handsome steer with an enormous spread of horns.

"We could draw straws for him," Gil suggested.

"Or better yet, our guns," Zack roared, whipping his six-gun out of its holster and shooting his younger brother dead.

When his temper abated, Zack was grief-stricken. He sadly lifted his brother's body and placed it tenderly over the back of a horse. A thoughtless cowhand asked how the steer should be branded now.

"With the same kind of brand that's on my hide," Zack sobbed. "Brand him Murder and cut him loose, and I hope to God he haunts the mesa for 1,000 years!"

He buried his brother that afternoon and then killed himself.

A few months later the branded steer began to appear in widely separate parts of the countryside. Amazingly, many who had even a passing glimpse of him were fated to kill or be killed.

A cowboy saw him and told his two best friends about it. When they accused him of lying, he shot them both. Hours after sighting the maverick steer, a small rancher killed his brother-in-law in a family argument.

A runaway boy lost all desire to be a gunman when he met the steer on a lonely trail. In the nearest cowtown, he tried to surrender his guns to the marshal. Tragically, the marshal misinterpreted the gesture and shot him down.

It was believed that the steer had died and had become a ghost whose restless hooves were taking it across all borders. The physical description had changed, too. The steer was now a bull.

Lon Allan, a Montana rancher, said in 1920, "The brand across him looked big and red and not healed up the way it ought to be, not haired over at all. It looked as raw and cruel in the moonlight as on the day they burned it into the critter."

Allan had been a partner with his friend Cole Farrell in a small spread next to Faye Dow's D-Down ranch. Dow wanted their land and one night called on Allan when he knew Farrell was in town. He managed to convince Allan that his friend was making love to his girl.

Crazed with jealousy, Allan crouched in a midnight ambush with a six-gun in his hand. At the sound of hoofbeats on the trail, he braced himself to kill. But the thing that blundered into the moonlight wasn't Cole Farrell's horse. It was the bull branded Murder.

In a wild panic, Allan sent four bullets crashing into the creature's skull. The apparition looked at him sadly and drifted away.

Faye Dow heard the shots and gleefully rushed to the scene. As the plot became evident, there was a shoot-out in which Allan was wounded and Dow died with two bullets in him.

In the strange trial that followed, Allan took the stand in his own defence. And in defence of the bull.

It was true, he said, that he'd seen the phantom and had killed a man moments later. But his partner was riding toward the ranch, and if it hadn't been for the bull he'd have killed the wrong man. The jury took ten minutes to acquit Allan.

The ghostly bull with the scarlet brand faded into history, for no one ever saw him again.

The witch's mark

Scars on a persecutor's grave

The year was 1692, and 13 people had been hanged for witchcraft in Salem, Massachusetts. It was a matter of concern to Colonel Bucks, of Bucksport, Maine, that his own village should be just as vigilant in stamping out witches. He raised the question repeatedly at town hall meetings. Shortly his one-man crusade produced a victim.

There was a public accusation of a bent and withered old lady who looked every inch a witch. Historians disagree as to her name and age, but one of them calls her Comfort Ainsworth and is sure she was more than 90 years old.

Because of her obvious frailty, the old lady went on trial without torture or pricking with needles to find "the witch's mark". But the crowds that surged into the courtroom knew her guilt had been predetermined by Colonel Bucks himself, who sat within whispering distance of the magistrate. When

---

Gallows curse

Norfolk Island, a dot in the Pacific Ocean 900 miles off the east coast of Australia, was a British penal colony until the last century, and many residents today claim to have seen the spectres of convicts hanged there.

But the strangest mystery is the legend of Barney Duffy's curse. The giant Irishman escaped from the colony's jail, and was found hiding in a hollow tree by two soldiers. Duffy knew he would be executed if returned to the prison.

He warned the privates: "If you take me back, you will die violently within a week of my hanging."

The two men ignored the threat, and Duffy died on the gallows. Two days later, the soldiers went fishing from a beach near the tree where they had captured him. Next morning, their beaten bodies were washed up by the tide. No one ever discovered who, or what, had killed them.

---

witnesses took the stand against her, without exception they looked to Bucks for approval.

One woman said she had heard the old woman muttering something that sounded gibberish. But when she reached home and her ears started bleeding, she knew it had been a curse.

A man swore he'd seen a black-garbed figure ten feet tall – obviously the devil or one of his henchmen – standing in Comfort's doorway.

The jury quickly returned a verdict of guilty. Quoting the text, "Thou shalt not suffer a witch to live," the judge denounced Comfort Ainsworth and sentenced her to hang next day.

No one was prepared for the scene that followed. Because she had not been permitted to testify in her own defence, people had assumed that the toothless old woman would remain mute.

Before the bailiffs could stop her, she got to her feet and pointed a bony finger at the colonel. "In all of my life," she screamed, "I have cursed no other being! But I am capable of laying a curse on you, sir, because you and your toadies have lied me to the gallows!

"Then mark you this, and mark it well – when you go to your grave, which will be soon, I pledge you I shall leave the print of my foot on your gravestone. And the print, Colonel Bucks, will be there forever so that the world can never forget this day!"

A bailiff clapped his palm to her mouth and carried her from the courtroom. But her words left the village uneasy, and there were few spectators when she was hanged next morning. Even Colonel Bucks failed to appear.

Three months later, he died from a "wasting disease", and the colonel's heirs found he had written a new instruction into his will. His headstone must be of the most flawless marble, "incapable of being stained or besmirched".

But in a few days the relatives were secretly approached by a terrified cemetery worker. He had found a woman's footprint in the marble, and no amount of sanding could remove it.

A new stonecutter was sworn to absolute secrecy. Working in the dead of night, he cut a marker that was an absolute replica of the first. The old stone was buried secretly and the new one raised.

Ten days later, the heirs saw crowds of frightened people moving in and out of the cemetery. Joining them, they found that the trick had failed. The shape of an old woman's narrow stockinged foot was clearly visible in the new stone.

Publicly deploring the phenomenon as an act of "graveyard vandalism" – an explanation that convinced no one – the heirs had a still more costly headstone hauled to the cemetery. It was raised with no attempt at secrecy. Incredibly, the print of Comfort's bony little foot soon began to take shape in the stone.

This time his discouraged heirs made no effort to replace the marker. Nearly three centuries later it stands over the grave of Colonel Bucks, the footprint still scarring its surface like a wound that will never heal.

The skulls of Calgarth

Wealthy Myles Phillipson owned huge tracts of the picturesque English Lake District countryside around Windermere, during the 16th century. But he was never satisfied with the extent of his empire, always restlessly seeking new acres to add to his estates. He eyed the small farm of Kraster and Dorothy Cook, which overlooked the lake. And he decided that their humble plot of land would be the ideal site for the new luxurious mansion he planned.

The farm was all the Cooks had in the world, and they were not prepared to sell when Phillipson made his offer. He was not a man to take no for an answer. He invited the poor couple to share Christmas dinner with him and his family. The Cooks were awed by the foods and wines, and overjoyed when the landowner said they could keep a golden bowl they admired.

Next morning, soldiers hammered at the door of their home, and arrested them. For a week they were held in separate cells, with no idea why they were being imprisoned. Only when they arrived in court did they learn of their "crime" – stealing a golden bowl from Myles Phillipson.

The verdict was a foregone conclusion, because the magistrate hearing the case was Phillipson himself. When he sentenced them both to death, Dorothy Cook cried out: "Look out for yourself, you will never prosper. The time will come when you own no land. You will never be rid of us ..."

Phillipson was not worried by the threats. The couple were hustled to the gallows, and strung up to die.

Within days, Phillipson had acquired their land and started work on his magnificent new home, called Calgarth Hall. When it was finished, he held a lavish Christmas feast to celebrate. Friends and neighbours joined him round the table, making merry with no expense spared.

Then a terrifying scream sent them rushing upstairs, swords at the ready.

Phillipson's wife stood halfway up the staircase, shuddering as she stared transfixed at a hideous sight on the bannister – two grinning skulls. The landowner seized them, threw them into the courtyard, and swore revenge on whoever had perpetrated the tasteless joke.

But his threats failed to put the minds of his guests at rest. Several shuffled

The restless skull

Collecting skulls was the private passion of a British doctor, John Kilner. He had them specially polished and encased in ebony boxes which he displayed round his home. But the skull that fascinated him most of all was one he did not own. It was on a skeleton at West Suffolk Hospital, where he worked in the 1870s.

Part of the attraction was the skeleton's gruesome history. It was the skeleton of a murderer, 23-year-old William Corder, hanged in public at nearby Bury St Edmunds Prison, in April 1828, for the notorious Red Barn murder of Maria Marten.

For years, Dr Kilner greedily eyed the skeleton, which was used to teach students. Then, one night, he stole it and put it in one of the showcases in his home.

Immediately, his life became a nightmare. An evil spirit roamed the house muttering and breathing heavily; often, sobbing was heard. Eventually, a vivid white hand floated through the air and smashed the skull's showcase.

The doctor was so horrified that he gave the skull to a friend, who was in turn subjected to so much similar terror, that he finally gave it a Christian burial. The tormented soul of killer Corder was at last able to rest in peace.

off to bed early – only to be woken in the small hours by more screams. The skulls were back on the stairs.

Over the next few days, Phillipson tried everything he knew to get rid of them. But each time they were thrown outside or buried, the skulls returned to haunt the home.

Christmas was ruined. And as the news spread, so was Phillipson. His business declined, his riches dwindled. When he died, a broken man, his beautiful home rang all night with the demonic laughter of the skulls.

The two gruesome relics continued to visit the hall, giving the landowner's heirs no rest. They appeared each Christmas Day, and on the anniversary of the Cooks' execution. Only when the family became too poor to maintain Calgarth, and were forced to sell it, did the skulls leave the building in peace.

Possessed!

Take-over by the last witch

Terry Palmer set out to find the resting place of the last witch in England to be burned at the stake. But his quest took him along an unnerving path – with his own body taken over by the witch he sought.

The spirit said she would be with Terry for all time, no matter where he went.

England's last witch, whose name was Elsa, was tortured and burned to death on the old village green of Dedham, Essex, in 1763. More than 200 years later Terry set out to find her burial place. But everywhere he went, inexplicable happenings took place.

He once visited a former convent where a terrier dog ran out to greet him, barking and wagging its tail. Then it ran back to its master, before bounding back – right past Terry. It was barking and leaping at an empty space.

A few days later in a shop, another dog barked twice at Terry ... and then twice at the empty space behind him.

The extraordinary tale of Terry, a good, book publisher, began when he went to a seance on his witch-hunting trail. There, says Terry, Elsa herself took over his body and joined in the ghost hunt.

Shortly afterwards, his father became possessed by evil spirits, and a fire broke out in his factory causing thousands of pounds of damage.

Terry claimed to have found Elsa's grave, near an hotel not far from the tiny village where she was executed. He stood on the spot and felt a tingling sensation from the back of his head to the middle of his spine. But when he and a friend dug down they found nothing.

Terry's story was told in the hotel and was treated with scepticism – until one day when a barman was having lunch while keeping an eye on the empty bar through a mirror. He saw a woman standing in the room and went to serve her. But the bar was empty, and all the doors were locked.

The Duke's grief

York Villa, the building in historic Bath that now houses a bus company's social club, has had several supernatural visitors over the years.

A young boy, a lady in grey, and a man in a long cloak have all been seen and footsteps have been heard walking upstairs.

All the ghostly happenings are said to date back to the time when the house was the home of one of the mistresses of Frederick, Duke of York, the son of George III. When he left for London after telling her their affair was over, the mistress decided to follow him, instructing her servants to take care of her two children.

But the staff had not been paid for some time, and left the house. When one old retainer returned some days later, he found the two children starved to death. The footsteps sadly climbing the stairs are said to be his.

Skyway to doom

Has the ghost of an American construction worker put a curse on the Sunshine Skyway Bridge? That was the theory put forward by a Florida fisherman after nearly 60 people died in four separate shipping disasters at the Tampa Bay bridge during the first five months of 1980.

In January, 23 coastguards were killed when their cutter collided with an oil tanker. The following month, a freighter smashed into one of the main bridge supports, and ten days later a tanker ran out of control, and slammed into the main span.

But the worst accident to hit the jinxed bridge came on May 9. Possibly blinded by the wind-lashed rain of a violent storm, the skipper of a 10,000-

ton Liberian freighter, *Summit Venture*, misjudged his approach to the bridge. Instead of passing under the middle of it, the ship ploughed into one of the main supports, and a huge section of the road running over it collapsed.

Cars, trucks and a Greyhound bus plunged 150 feet into the water; 32 people died, 23 of them on the bus. Other drivers missed death by inches, slamming on their brakes just in time as the yawning gap opened up in front of them.

The Florida House of Representatives stood for a moment's silence as news of the tragedy reached them during a meeting. One member blamed the Tampa Bay harbour pilot system, and called for an inquiry.

But a local fisherman, 27-year-old Charlie Williams, said later: "When the bridge was being built, a construction worker fell into some wet concrete. He's still there, in the structure. The Skyway has been cursed ever since."

The bridge, which is four miles long, was opened in September 1954. More than 40 people have committed suicide by leaping from it.

Chapter Two

Haunted Homes

From the outside they look perfectly normal.
Nothing strikes the casual visitor as strange. But the
people who really know the picturesque castles,
stately mansions and seemingly-ordinary houses
have different stories to tell. They have experienced
the uneasiness of unexplained noises, the shock of
inanimate objects flying through the air for no
reason, the terror of unreal and unearthly sights.
They have experienced a haunted home . . .

House of evil

Amityville jinx hit actor

Actor James Brolin is certain there was an evil jinx on the film *The Amityville Horror*, in which he starred. He played surveyor George Lutz who, with his family, was driven from his home by a terrifying series of demonic happenings. The film was based on the best-selling book by Jay Anson, to whom the Lutz family told their nightmare story.

Brolin said: "On the first day of filming I stepped into the elevator in my apartment block and pressed the button for the lobby floor. Before we'd gone three floors it shuddered to a grinding, screeching halt, the lights flickered and I was plunged into frightening darkness. I screamed for help but nobody could hear me.

"It was an eerie, frightening experience. You imagine all sorts of hair-raising things in the silent darkness. My pleas bounced back like an echo. Those 30 minutes seemed an eternity."

The jinx hit again the next morning. "I'd been on the set less than one minute when I tripped over a cable and severely wrenched my ankle," said Brolin. "I hobbled around in pain for days."

The film recorded the horrifying events experienced by George and Kathleen Lutz and their three children after they moved to Long Island, New York, to a house which had been the scene of a multiple murder in 1974.

Ronald Defoe, 23-year-old son of a wealthy car dealer, had drugged his parents, brothers and sisters at supper and at 3.15 am, he stalked from room to room shooting each victim in the back with a rifle.

He claimed in court that "voices" had ordered him to commit the crime. Defoe was sentenced to six consecutive life sentences.

For the Lutzes, the house's macabre history gave them the chance to buy a dream home at the bargain price of $80,000. Seen in the bright light of day, it was a beautiful, three-storied colonial-style residence, set on a well-kept lawn which sloped gently down to the bay, and its own boathouse. In the small, middle-class community of Amityville it was a showplace.

Soon after the family moved in they asked the local priest, Father Mancuso (played in the film by Rod Steiger) to bless the house. Author Anson wrote: "The priest entered the house to begin his ritual. When he flicked the first holy water and uttered the words that accompany the gesture, Father Mancuso heard a masculine voice say with terrible clarity, 'Get out!'

"He looked up in shock, but he was alone in the room. Who or whatever

A still from the film *The Amityville Horror* showing the Lutz's house.

had spoken was nowhere to be seen."

For the first two nights in their new home, the Lutzes were awakened by strange noises at 3.15 am. But the real horror began on the third night.

As usual, George Lutz checked that all doors and windows were locked before going to bed. The noises roused him again at 3.15, and this time he went downstairs to investigate.

He could not believe what he saw. The heavy, solid-wood front door had been wrenched open and was hanging by one hinge. With mounting terror he realised it had been forced from inside the house. The thick steel doorknob spindle was twisted, and the surrounding metal plate had been forced outwards.

From then on, the house seemed to have an evil life of its own. Windows opened and closed at will and a bannister was wrenched from the staircase.

Two weeks after the front-door incident. George woke in the night to find his wife Kathleen floating above the bed. George pulled Kathleen down by her hair and switched on the light. He was looking not at his attractive young wife, but at a hideous vision.

Kathleen caught a glimpse of her reflection in a mirror and screamed:

"That's not me. It can't be me!" Her appearance changed slowly back to normal over the next six hours.

A few nights later Kathleen was in the sitting room with George when she looked up and saw two glowing red eyes at the darkened window. She and George hurried outside and found strange tracks in the snow. Kathleen told Anson: "The prints had been left by cloven hooves – like those of an enormous pig."

After only 28 days the Lutzes fled the dream house that had become a nightmare.

As they hurriedly gathered a few belongings, amid a series of unearthly noises, green slime oozed from the walls and ceiling and a sticky black substance dripped from the keyholes.

Because of the curse, the film men dared not use the actual house. They found an almost identical building in New Jersey. They knew only too well of the frightening things that had happened to people connected with the story.

A photographer went to take pictures of Anson immediately after photographing the Amityville house. While he was in the author's home, his car caught fire and billowed orange smoke as it stood empty with the engine switched off.

Anson himself told of terrifying events linked with his book. He said: "A woman to whom I loaned some early chapters took the manuscript home. She and two of her children were suffocated in a fire that night. The only item in the apartment that was not damaged by the fire was the manuscript.

"Another man put the manuscript in the trunk of his car and attempted to drive home. He drove through what he thought was a puddle. It turned out to be a 12-foot-deep hole into which his car slid. When the car was fished out the next day, the only dry object in it was the manuscript.

"And when my editor picked up the completed manuscript at my office his car caught fire and he discovered that all the bolts on his engine had been loosened."

Anson himself suffered a heart attack, and his son and friend were nearly killed in a car smash.

The Lutzes are today alive and well in California, and planning another book about their experiences. Their Long Island house of horrors is now owned by James and Barbara Cromarty.

They say the place is not haunted.

Whatever the truth, the movie *The Amityville Horror*, will remain a chillingly realistic record of paranormal events. Director Stuart Rosenberg says that he would not have taken on the project if it was just another horror film.

He insists, "My first reaction was that it wouldn't be my cup of tea. But I read Jay Anson's book – and it had the ring of truth about it."

Torment of Calvados

Diaries chart a castle nightmare

Diaries written by a French aristocrat who lived in a gloomy mediaeval castle set among the apple orchards of Normandy tell the story of one of the most violent hauntings ever recorded. Known simply as X, he recorded in vivid detail the extraordinary events that turned his historic home into a nightmare in the year 1875.

They began without warning. Everyone in Calvados Castle had settled down for the night when they were disturbed by ghostly wailing and weeping and rapping on the walls. The noises were heard by the entire household – X himself, his wife, his son, his son's tutor who was an abbé, Emile the coachman, and servants Auguste, Amelina and Celina.

After several nights of ever-increasing noise and disturbance, the aristocrat instructed that fine threads were to be strung across every entrance to the castle. He hoped, of course, that in the morning they would be broken, proving that someone had entered and was trying to terrorise them.

But the threads remained intact. There was no escaping the fact that the forces existed within the castle walls.

On Wednesday, October 13, 1875, X began keeping a diary. That night the abbé was alone in his room when he heard a series of sharp taps on the wall and a candlestick on the mantlepiece was lifted by an unseen hand.

The terror-stricken priest rang for X who found that not only had the candlestick been moved, but also an armchair which was normally fixed to the floor.

For the next two days, pounding on the walls, footsteps on the stairs and other un-nerving phenomena continued unabated. X and the abbé armed themselves with sticks and searched the castle from top to bottom. They could find no human explanation.

By October 31 the castle was hardly ever at peace. X recorded in his diary, "A very disturbed night. It sounded as if someone went up the stairs with superhuman speed from the ground floor, stamping his feet.

"Arriving on the landing, he gave five heavy blows so strong that objects rattled in their places. Then it seemed as if a heavy anvil or a big log had been thrown at the wall so as to shake the house.

"Nobody could say where the blows came from, but everyone got up and assembled in the hall. The house only settled down at about three in the morning ..."

The following night everyone was awakened by what sounded like a heavy body rolling downstairs followed by blows so ferocious they seemed to rock the castle. Over the next few days, the haunting had become so violent the family felt it could not possibly get any worse. But greater ordeals were to come.

On the night of November 10, X wrote in his diary, "Everyone heard a long shriek and then another as of a woman outside calling for help. At 1.45 we suddenly heard three or four loud cries in the hall and then on the staircase."

Cries, screams and moans which "sounded like the cries of the damned" seemed to fill the whole castle. Heavy furniture was moved, windows flung open and – more terrifying – Bibles were torn and desecrated. The family began to wonder if the powers of darkness had taken over.

X's wife suddenly became the focus of attention. Hearing a noise in the abbé's room, she crept up the stairs and put out a hand to press down the latch on the door. Before she could touch it she saw the key turn in the lock

---

Face in the floor

One of the world's most puzzling ghost stories began on an afternoon in August, 1971, in a cottage in the Spanish village of Belmez, near Cordoba, in Andalucia.

An old woman was busy in the kitchen, preparing the evening meal, when her grandchild started to scream. The grandmother turned from her oven – and saw a tormented face stare up at her from the faded pink tiles of the kitchen floor.

When she tried to rub the vision out with a rag, the eyes opened wider, making the expression of the face even more heart-rending.

The woman sent for the owner of the house. He ripped up the tiles and replaced them with concrete. But three weeks later another face began to form in the new surface, even more clearly defined than the first.

The owner called in the authorities, who excavated one section of the floor, and found what seemed to be the remains of a mediaeval burial ground.

The floor was repaired, but soon faces started appearing all over the carefully-laid concrete; first one, then another, then a whole group.

The kitchen was locked and sealed off, but faces began to appear in other parts of the house. Investigators moved in with ultra-sensitive microphones, and picked up agonised moans and voices speaking in a strange language, sounds undetectable to the human ear.

But before anyone could discover what they were, and why they were there, the faces and sounds just melted away, as suddenly and as mysteriously as they had arrived.

then remove itself, hitting her left hand with a sharp blow. The abbé, who had run up the stairs after her, saw it happen and afterwards testified that madame's hand was bruised for two days. That night something hammered on her door so furiously she thought it would break down.

The New Year brought only fresh terrors to the wretched family: louder knocking, more persistent voices. The worst day of all was January 26 when the noise was thunderous. "It sounded as if demons were driving herds of wild cattle through the rooms." Peals of demonic laughter rang through the ancient walls. The family had had enough.

Next day a priest was called in to exorcise the evil spirit and the family saw to it that every religious medallion and relic they possessed was placed in full view. The treatment was effective and at last the hideous uproar ceased.

To the family, who believed they would be forced to abandon their home, the peace that followed came as a blessed relief.

But the ghostly tormentors of Calvados had not quite finished. Shortly after the exorcism, all the religious relics disappeared and could not be found. Then, one morning, as the lady of the house sat writing at her desk an unseen hand dropped them one by one in front of her. There was one short burst of violent sound, then silence.

The haunting of Willington Mill

Phantoms in the Quakers' house

When Joseph Procter and his family moved into the mill house in 1835 they paid little attention to rumours that the place was haunted. The house was a pleasant, comparatively new building set by a tidal stream in the Northumberland village of Willington, in England's rugged north-east. The Procters were a highly-respected, devoutly Quaker family. Mr Procter was said to be a man of high intelligence and common sense, good and kind to his family and employees.

Yet after little more than a decade, the Procters were driven to leave in distress, unable to stand any more of the weird and ghostly happenings that plagued them from the day they first arrived at Willington Mill.

Invisible incline

James Herrmann could not believe his eyes as he brushed his teeth one night in February, 1958. A bottle of medicine slid 18 inches along a perfectly level shelf in front of him. Within days, bottles of shampoo and holy water were uncapping themselves and spilling their contents.

When porcelain figures and a glass bowl were smashed after flying through the air for no apparent reason, Mr Herrmann called the police to the house in Long Island, New York.

A baffled officer reported: "Something weird is happening there."

Only much later were they to learn that their house had been built on the site of an old cottage, that a terrible crime had been committed there years before ... and that a priest had refused to hear the confession of a woman who desperately wanted to unburden her conscience.

So prolific was the haunting of Willington Mill while the Procters lived there that when W T Stead, the writer and ghost hunter, first pieced together the story in the 1890s, there were still 40 people alive who had actually seen the ghosts.

The hauntings began one night in January 1835. A nursemaid was putting the children to bed in the second-floor nursery when she heard heavy footsteps coming from a room immediately above. It was an empty room, never used by the family. At first the girl took little notice, thinking it must be one of the handymen with a job to do. But they went on night after night, getting louder and louder.

Other servants and members of the family also heard them, but when they burst into the room to surprise the "intruder", no one was there. They sprinkled meal over the floor, but there were no footprints.

One morning, as Mr Procter was conducting family prayers, the heavy steps were heard coming down the stairs, past the parlour and along the hall to the front door. The family heard the bar removed, two bolts drawn back and the lock turned.

Mr Procter rushed into the hall to find the door open. The footsteps went on down the path.

Poor Mrs Procter fainted.

It became increasingly difficult to get servants to stay in the house. Only one girl, Mary Young, whom the family had brought with them from their previous home in North Shields, loyally refused to leave.

There was a period when it seemed as though the whole house had been taken over by unseen people. There were sounds of doors opening, people entering and leaving rooms, thumps and blows and laboured breathing, the steps of a child, chairs being moved and rustling sounds as if a woman in a silk dress was hurrying by.

Until a certain Whit Monday, the haunting remained entirely by sound. On that day, Mary Young was washing dishes in the kitchen when she heard footsteps in the passage. Looking up she saw a woman in a lavender silk dress go upstairs and enter one of the rooms. That night the noises in the house were worse than anybody had heard before.

Two of Mrs Procter's sisters arrived for a visit. The first night, sleeping together in the same four-poster bed, they felt it lift up. Their first thought was that a thief had hidden there, so they rang the alarm and the men of the house came running. No one was found.

On another night their bed was violently shaken and the curtains suddenly hoisted up then let down again several times.

They had the curtains removed, but the experience that followed was even more terrifying. They lay awake half-expecting something to happen when a misty, bluish figure of a woman drifted out of the wall and leaned over them in an almost horizontal position. Both women saw the figure quite clearly and lay there, speechless with terror, as it retreated and passed back into the wall.

Neither would sleep in the room another night and one of them even left the house to take lodgings with mill foreman Thomas Mann and his wife.

One dark, moonless night the Manns, their daughter and their visitor were walking past the mill house after paying a call on neighbours. All four saw the luminous figure of what appeared to be a priest in a surplice gliding back and forth at the height of the second floor. It seemed to go through the wall of the house and stand looking out of the window.

The focus of the hauntings seemed to be what the Procters called The Blue Room and in the summer of 1840 they agreed to allow Edward Drury, who specialised in supernatural investigation, to spend a night there. He took with him a friend who refused to get into bed, but dozed off in a chair.

Drury later wrote a letter describing what happened. "I took out my watch to ascertain the time and found that it wanted ten minutes to one," he said. "In taking my eyes off the watch they became riveted upon a closet door, which I distinctly saw open, and saw also the figure of a female attired in greyish garments, with the head inclining downwards and one hand pressed upon the chest as if in pain. It advanced with an apparently cautious step across the floor towards me. Immediately, it approached my friend, who was slumbering, its right hand extended towards him. I then rushed at it . . ."

It was three hours before Drury could recollect anything more. He had been carried downstairs in a state of terror by Mr Procter. Drury had shrieked, "There she is. Keep her off. For God's sake, keep her off!"

The grey lady was seen by others. So were unearthly animals and other startling apparitions. The Procters tried to shield their children from the worst of the haunting, but eventually they became involved. One day a daughter told Mary Young, "There's a lady sitting on the bed in mama's room. She has eyeholes, but no eyes, and she looked hard at me."

Then another daughter reported that in the night a lady had come out of the wall and looked into the mirror ... "She had eyeholes, but no eyes."

Another child saw the figure of a man enter his room, push up the sash window, lower it again, then leave.

In 1847 Joseph Procter decided his family could endure no more. They moved away to another part of Northumberland and were never again troubled by ghosts.

The house was later divided into two dwellings and eventually deteriorated into a slum. People continued to hear and see strange things from time to time. But Willington Mill House was never again to know the terrifying days and nights that afflicted the pious Quaker family.

Knock twice for terror

From the outside, it looked like any house. But the many people called in to investigate the strange happenings there knew differently. Journalists, psychic investigators, even the police, came to the same conclusion: the rented house in the North London suburb of Enfield, occupied by Mrs Peggy Hodgson and her four children, was haunted.

It all began in September 1977, when daughter Janet, then 11, heard a shuffling noise in her bedroom. It sounded like someone walking in loose-fitting slippers. Four loud knocks followed and Janet was horrified to see a heavy chest of drawers sliding away from the wall.

In the days that followed, other objects, including a heavy bed, began to move unaided. A hairbrush flew through the air hitting one of the sons on the head. A policewoman, who was called, saw a chair hurled across a room.

But fright turned to terror as the thing that haunted the house extended its powers and started to influence the children's behaviour. The girls, both in their early teens, spoke in coarse language with the voices of old men. But their lips did not move – the sounds just seemed to come from within them.

It also appeared that the children's lives could be in danger. Mrs

The terrified Hodgson family, hosts to a poltergeist.

GHOSTS

Hodgson's nine-year-old son Billy escaped narrowly when a heavy iron grate flew across his room as he lay in bed. As Janet lay asleep, she would suddenly find herself hurled into the air to wake screaming.

On one occasion the strange force nearly killed Janet. As she lay in bed, a nearby curtain wrapped itself tight around her neck. Hearing her daughter's choking scream. Mrs Hodgson rushed to the room and fought to pull the material from the girl's neck.

The family considered moving away from their home, but for a divorcée with four children such a step was not easy. And the family feared that "the thing" might follow them, for there had been strange voices and happenings when they were on holiday in a caravan at Clacton, Essex.

Many of those who heard of the family's plight were quick to dismiss it all as childish pranks, but not so the experts. Pye Electronics specialists who visited the house were baffled to find that video recording equipment which worked perfectly well outside would not function at all inside.

A policewoman who was called in admitted: "I saw a chair lift into the air. It moved sideways and then floated back to its original position. I have been called to the house several times, but there isn't much the police can do."

Psychical researcher Maurice Grosse tried communicating with "the thing" using a code of one knock for No, two knocks for Yes.

"Did you die in the house?"

Two knocks.

"How many years did you live here?"

Fifty-three knocks.

This was followed by a barrage of knocks. Bewildered, Grosse asked: "Are you having a game with me?"

In answer, a cardboard box filled with cushions leaped off the floor hitting him on the head.

It was Janet's sister Margaret who shed some light on what was happening. One night when she was asleep, she began to bounce up and down in bed and cried: "Go away, you ten little things."

Still asleep, she gave details about them. They included a baby, three girls, two boys and an elderly couple one of whom she identified as Frank Watson, "the man who died in the chair downstairs."

Then frightening, throaty growls began to come from Janet's direction, but investigators were convinced she could not have made the sounds herself.

One day the voice told researcher Grosse that its name was Joe, and on another day, Bill Hobbs. He said he came from Durant's Park graveyard.

Hobbs, whose voice was being taped, told them: "I am 72 years old and I have come here to see my family. But they are not here now."

The hauntings lasted three years, and then ended, never to resume.

The spinster's grave
How Hannah returned to guard her gold

Spinster Hannah Beswick died more than 200 years ago. Her body was embalmed, but her restless spirit still haunts a factory built on the land where her home once stood.

Hannah was a wealthy Lancashire landowner whose house, Birchen Bower, dominated acres of fertile land at Hollinwood, on the outskirts of Manchester. She was not normally fearful, but when in 1745 Bonnie Prince Charlie crossed the border into England and advanced south, she became so obsessed with the thought of the invading Scots that she hid all her money and valuables. They remained hidden for the rest of her life.

Apart from the Scots, her only real terror was that of being buried alive – a fear quite understandable in the light of what had happened in her own family. One of her brothers had fallen ill and, while unconscious, had been pronounced dead by a local doctor. Preparations were made for his funeral and he was laid in an open coffin so that friends and relatives could pay their last respects. While lying in his shroud surrounded by flowers he began to show signs of life. The unfortunate man was hastily removed to his bed.

Hannah died in 1768 without divulging where she had hidden her fortune. Because of what had happened to her brother, she took steps to ensure that her corpse was not buried.

She left Birchen Bower to young Doctor Charles White with the stipulation that he must have her embalmed and kept in a safe and respectable place above ground.

For some strange reason, she also insisted that every 21 years her body

---

A professor's warning

Night classes for ghost-hunters proved so popular at Glasgow University that four times the expected number of people enrolled. Students on the 10-week course included clergymen, accountants and senior citizens.

Professor Archie Roy, the university's head of astronomy, a keen amateur ghost detective, told his students: "My aim is to open minds to great mysteries. But I also warn of the dangers."

The scientist, a leading authority on ghosts, is often called in to investigate weird happenings, and spends his holidays seeking out old haunts.

should be taken back to the house and allowed to lie in the granary for seven days.

Old Hannah was duly mummified, her body coated with tar and wrapped in heavy linen bandages. In accordance with her wishes, the face was left uncovered.

For many years Dr White faithfully kept the body at his own home, Sale Priory, but when he died it was moved to Manchester Natural History Society's museum where it became a major attraction.

A century after Hannah Beswick was embalmed, the commissioners of the society, finding the museum over-filled with relics and needing room for new acquisitions, decided it was time she was given a proper burial. She was finally interred at Harpurhey Cemetery on July 22, 1868.

Some people had already claimed to have seen her ghost wandering through the rooms of Birchen Bower, dressed in her usual black silk gown and white lace cap. After burial the ghost became more agitated. Hannah was seen hurrying between the old barn and the pond as though deeply troubled. Sometimes, it was said, the old barn glowed as if on fire.

The house remained empty for some years, inhabited only by the spirit of Hannah Beswick. Then it was bought by a developer, renovated and converted into small dwellings to be rented out to cotton workers and labourers. The new tenants were often to see her drifting by, head bent as though in deep thought.

One particular aspect of her behaviour was puzzling. Sometimes she would disappear at a particular spot – a corner flagstone in the parlour of a house occupied by a handloom weaver. Hannah seemed to hover about this room as though reluctant to leave it.

The weaver decided to pull up part of the flagstone floor to make a place where he could install a new loom. To his amazement he found hidden underneath a hoard of gold. He had found part of Hannah Beswick's fortune.

After this, Hannah was seen frequently ... no longer thoughtful but angry and menacing. People spoke of a brilliant blue light darting from her eyes. Sometimes at night she was seen near the pond and at other times strange unearthly noises were heard in the barn. No one would venture there after dark unless they had urgent business.

It gave rise to the speculation that perhaps the rest of her valuables were hidden nearby and she was determined to protect them.

The hauntings continued until Birchen Bower was demolished. A factory was built on the spot and that was thought to be the end of the affair.

Then, people who knew nothing of her story began saying that they had caught a glimpse of a strange old world figure in a black silk gown and white lace cap ...

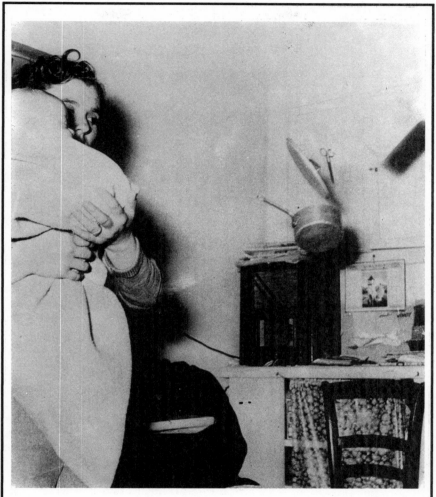

The French photographer from *Samedi Soir*, who captured this remarkable event, prepared his picture well. He asked everyone except the tenants to leave the room in which it was said a poltergeist gave frightening performances. After waiting patiently for 1½ hours a strange knock heralded these events. A saucepan and its lid, a pair of scissors and a telegraph form flew into the air. Gerrard Lestienne, photographer, guarantees his pictures are not faked.

John Wesley's nightmare
Poltergeist tests a family's faith

John Wesley

The servant who answered a knock on the door of a Lincolnshire parsonage was mildly annoyed to find no one there when he opened it. He blamed playful youngsters, but when, only hours later, he watched a corn-grinding handmill turning without human help, he realised that something beyond his understanding was happening.

The events of that December day in 1716 heralded a two-month nightmare for the devout household at Epworth. Their ordeal was chronicled by one of the family's children – John Wesley, who was to become founder of the Methodist Church.

His sister Molly was the next person to notice something strange. As she sat reading in the library, the door opened on its own, and she heard footsteps walking round her chair, accompanied by the rustling of petticoats.

One by one, the rest of the family told of their own eerie experiences: rappings on a table, mysterious footsteps on the stairs, bangs in the hall and kitchen, the sound of an invisible cradle rocking in the nursery.

At 9.45 each evening, a man's steps were heard plodding down from the north-east corner of the house. The Wesleys christened him Old Jeffrey.

John's father Samuel became convinced that the spirit was an agent of evil testing the faith of the family. Finally he challenged it to leave the children alone, and meet him alone in the study for a showdown. It was to be a spectacular confrontation.

When Mr Wesley tried to enter the room, a powerful force pushed the door back in his face. He struggled through and began asking the phantom to identify itself. His questions were answered only by furious knocking from each wall in turn, building to a terrifying crescendo.

But the parson's faith and nerve were unshakable. Gradually the spirit's apparent anger subsided, the sounds faded, and the house was left in peace.

The Epworth haunting is one of the best-documented cases of poltergeists, ghosts that are heard but not seen. They are more common than spirits that materialise, and in many ways even more frightening.

The word poltergeist is derived from German, where the earliest cases were reported. In 355 AD, people in the village of Bingen-am-Rhein were hauled from their beds by unseen hands, and subjected to an onslaught of stones and strange noises. Five centuries later, the same thing happened at nearby Kembden, when a disembodied voice accused the local priest and some of the villagers of misdeeds.

In 1721, the Groben home of German Oriental scholar Professor Schupart was invaded by an invisible terror which threw furniture about. His wife was bitten, pinched and knocked down, and the professor was violently assaulted by an invisible attacker. Incredulous neighbours witnessed the incident.

Since then, poltergeists have been reported all over the world. In 1762, eminent men of letters such as Dr Samuel Johnson, Horace Walpole and Oliver Goldsmith were among those who investigated strange rappings and scratching at a house in London's Cock Lane.

And at Syderstone Rectory, in Norfolk, curious groans, slamming doors, running footsteps in corridors, and knocking that shook the whole house were reported by several families in a 40-year period that ended in 1833.

In 1890, Cesare Lombroso, a leading Italian psychiatrist was called in by the owners of a small inn at Turin. He watched bottles of wine smash and shoes fly through the air.

In 1937, stones and other missiles rained down for almost a week on a family in Port Louis, Mauritius – even when all doors and windows were bolted shut.

GHOSTS

One of the most terrifying poltergeists on record struck in 1878 at Amherst, Nova Scotia. Terrible crashes under the bed of 19-year-old Esther Cox were followed by lighted matches tumbling from the ceiling. Mystery fires flared up in the cellar of her home, and a dress went up in flames.

A doctor treating the girl for shock was pelted with plaster and planks of wood, and saw bedclothes being ripped off her bed. The family fled after a wall was daubed with the message: "Esther Cox, you are mine to kill."

Today, the invisible spirits are still getting up to mischief, often in the most unlikely places. In 1963, the day after motor cycle dealer Sid Mularney knocked down a wall in his workshops at Leighton Buzzard, Bedfordshire, he found three of his bikes damaged.

He then watched spanners fly off their hooks and a tarpaulin rise from a scooter and shoot across the room. Petrol tanks were mysteriously moved, and neighbours complained of weird nocturnal noises from the building.

A West German lawyer's office in Rosenheim, Bavaria, was suddenly plunged into chaos in November, 1967. Light bulbs started smashing for no reason and lamp shades tumbled to the ground. One day all four phones on the man's desk rang simultaneously, but there were no callers when he lifted the receivers. Experts who checked his premises reported sudden strange surges in the electricity current.

An American family found a quilt in a box when they moved into their new

On the left of the picture is Andrew Green, official ghost-hunter for Ben Truman, an English brewer. He is relaxing in his own pub but his job is investigating ghosts in Truman's pubs.

home in Poy Sippi, Wisconsin, in 1972, and decided to use it on their spare bed. But guests seldom slept soundly under it. They told their hostess, Mrs Dora Monroe, that someone kept tugging it off the bed during the night.

Mrs Monroe's daughter Florence said she was awakened at midnight, and during a battle to keep the quilt covering her, she heard a voice say: "Give me back my Christmas present."

The Foundation for Research into the Nature of Man, set up at Duke University, Carolina, in 1964, noted that poltergeist activity often stops when a teenager leaves the home or office. Some experts believe the manifestations may be caused by psychokinesis, an energy released during puberty which gives young minds power over matter.

The defiant spirit

A ghost which defied a priest's effort to exorcise it finally drove a young couple from their home.

Andy Ralph, his wife Julie and their seven-month-old baby Charlene quit the Victorian house in Sheerness, Kent. In Andy's words, "Our nerves finally cracked. Nothing would drive the spirit away."

Julie said, "We were horrified one evening when coins started flying into the room. They were coming from the stairwell and bouncing off the floor and walls of the sitting room. There was no explanation for it."

Apart from the case of the flying coins, the couple claimed that doors mysteriously slammed, light bulbs flicked on and off without anybody touching a switch, Julie felt a strangling sensation as she relaxed in an armchair, and sounds of someone gasping for breath, heavy footsteps and scraping noises were heard.

Andy and Julie, both aged 19, put up with the eerie incidents for five months. Eventually the phenomena became too alarming and they sought the help of a priest, who exorcised the old house. The exorcism failed, and within days the persistent spook was back.

If the ghost wouldn't budge, the Ralphs would, and in 1981 they quit, leaving a mystery that has not yet been solved.

Locals had one theory – Harry Morgan, a kindly man who had died alone in the house six years earlier and whose body had gone undiscovered for several days, may have been getting his own back on his "uncaring" neighbours.

The smiling spectre

The ghost of a tall woman, dressed in grey, sometimes mingles with tourists looking over Chambercombe Manor, near the North Devon holiday resort of Ilfracombe. She was seen as recently as 1976, and is usually reported with a smile on her face.

Which is surprising, for the story of her life and death is far from happy.

Alexander Oatway was one of the notorious West Country ship wreckers of 400 years ago. On stormy nights, he would leave his fireside at Chambercombe and hurry to the shore carrying a powerful lantern, which he used as a beacon to lure trusting ships seeking safe harbour on to the rocks, where he and his friends plundered them.

One wild night his son William followed him to the beach. The lantern trick worked yet again, but a young Spanish girl survived the wreck. William rescued her, took her home and fell in love. The couple married, and settled on Lundy Island, in the Bristol Channel, leaving Alexander to his deadly hobby. They had a daughter, Kate.

Nearly 20 years later, William heard that his old home was vacant, and decided to move back to it. The rent was high, but he could afford it. The household bills were lightened when Kate fell in love with an Irish sea captain called Wallace. He took her home to Dublin as his bride.

Years passed. Then one winter's night a vicious storm blew up. William hurried down to the beach below Chambercombe Manor after spotting a ship in trouble. He found a woman lying on the rocks, disfigured after being battered by the sea. He carried her home, but she died during the night.

As he checked her belongings, William fell to temptation. The woman was carrying a belt with enough money and jewellery to enable him to buy his beloved manor house outright. Two days later, a man from the Admiralty called, making inquiries about a missing passenger from the wrecked ship. William said he knew nothing about it. Then the visitor mentioned the name of the missing woman – Mrs Katherine Wallace.

William and his wife were devastated. They had stolen from their own dead daughter, her face unrecognisable because of the impact of the rocks. Filled with remorse, they walled her body in a secret room and moved away.

Their guilty secret was revealed 150 years later. In 1865 a farmer living in the house was busy re-thatching the roof when he looked down, and saw a skeleton lying on a cramped bed in a room he never knew existed. The walls were taken down, and the bones buried in a pauper's grave at Ilfracombe. But Kate's ghost still haunts her former home.

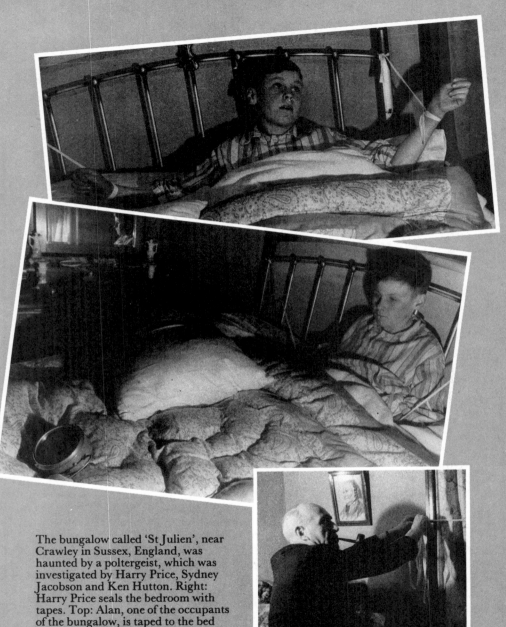

The bungalow called 'St Julien', near Crawley in Sussex, England, was haunted by a poltergeist, which was investigated by Harry Price, Sydney Jacobson and Ken Hutton. Right: Harry Price seals the bedroom with tapes. Top: Alan, one of the occupants of the bungalow, is taped to the bed while the investigation takes place. Above: The poltergeist causes the alarm clock to fly off the dressing table and land on the bed.

A mother's anguish

For nearly 400 years, the ghost of a woman dressed in mourning has been seen wandering the grounds of picturesque Bisham Abbey, near Marlow, Buckinghamshire seemingly washing her hands in a bowl which moves in front of her.

Two schoolboys also saw her once in a rowing boat on the river Thames, which flows at the foot of the mansion's lawns.

The pathetic figure is believed to be Dame Elizabeth Hoby, wife of a respected scholar, and close friend of Queen Elizabeth I. She wrote poetry in both Latin and English – she was over-ambitious for her children, forever urging them to greater efforts in their studies. But she despaired of her youngest son, William. Not only was he a slow learner, but his exercise books were full of ungrammatical sentences, misspelt words and ink blots. The intolerant mother gave him several beatings, but this did nothing to improve his work.

One morning, Dame Elizabeth was particularly exasperated. She cuffed the boy round the ears, ordered him to repeat the work he had done so badly and locked him in a cupboard until he had completed the task.

Then a messenger arrived from the Queen. She wanted Dame Elizabeth at court immediately. The mother left in a hurry – and forgot to tell her servants where William was. When she returned that evening, the boy was found dead, slumped over his books.

Until the day she died in 1609, at the age of 91, Dame Elizabeth never forgave herself.

In 1840, workmen moved into the Abbey buildings to carry out repairs. Between some Tudor floor joists, they found several books with a child's writing in them. One of the pages was blotted, but not with ink. The smudges were caused by long-dried tears.

QUEEN ELIZABETH.

Riddle of the Rectory

A dark gloomy mansion on the border between the English counties of Essex and Suffolk has been described as the world's most haunted house. And even though the building, Borley Rectory, burned down mysteriously in 1939, its legend lives on in strange happenings near the spot where it once stood.

The 23-room red-brick house was built in 1863 for the Reverend Henry Dawson Ellis Bull. As soon as he and his family moved in, they heard puzzling sounds at night. Footsteps and tappings were followed by bells ringing and voices answering. Ghostly chanting was heard from the nearby village church.

Soon the disturbances took on a more physical form. One of the 14 children in the family was awakened one day by a slap in the face. Another claimed to have seen a man in old-fashioned clothes standing by her bed. A nun, a phantom coach and horses, a headless man and a woman in white were all reported in the grounds by passers-by or servants.

In 1929 poltergeist activity began. Pebbles, keys and mementoes flew through the air for no apparent reason, and a cook told her master that a kitchen door locked each evening was inexplicably open when she arrived for work the following morning.

Just before the Bull family moved out, newspaper reporters kept vigil one night, and noted an eerie light in a deserted wing of the building.

The Reverend Lionel Algernon Foyster and his wife Marrianne moved into the Rectory in 1930, and the baffling incidents continued. Curious messages started appearing on walls or scraps of paper, urging: "Marrianne, get help."

Mrs Foyster also heard a disembodied voice call her name, and she was later attacked by an invisible assailant. Soon after that, the couple fled for a more peaceful home.

Ghost investigator Harry Price, founder of Britain's National Laboratory of Psychical Research, recruited a team of volunteers to document exactly what was happening at Borley. They reported sudden drops in temperature of up to ten degrees, curious incense-like smells, stones and cakes of soap thrown across rooms, and books moving as if of their own accord. A Benedictine monk trying to hold an exorcism in the Rectory was hit by flying pebbles.

When Captain W H Gregson bought the building, he re-named it Borley Priory. But the new name brought the jinxed home no better luck. In 1939 it

Excavations for the nun's skeleton or church plate said to be buried near Borley.

was wrecked by fire. Several people claimed that, as the flames raged, they saw a young girl at an upstairs window. Witnesses told the village policeman a grey-clad nun had been sighted slipping away from the inferno.

Even though the Rectory was destroyed, arguments about its ghosts raged on. Some said they were the spirits of a monk and a nun who had eloped from nearby Bures centuries before, but had suffered the traditional punishment when caught – decapitation for him, being buried alive for her.

But London medium Helen Glanville claimed that during a 1937 seance at her home in Streatham, she was told that the Borley ghost was that of Marie Lairre, a nun induced to leaver her convent at Le Havre, France, to marry one of the Waldergrave family from Borley Manor. She was strangled by him in May, 1667 – on the site where the Rectory was built.

In 1943, excavations of the ruins revealed fragments of a woman's skull and skeleton four feet below ground, together with a number of religious pendants. Were they the bones of unhappy Marie, or were they, as some suggested, the remains of a plague victim from even earlier times?

The Rectory may be long gone, but its supernatural residents outlasted it for many years. Chauffeur Herbert Mayes heard the thunder of invisible hooves as he drove past the shell of the building. During World War Two, air raid wardens were called to the ruins several times when lights were reported at windows. And as late as 1961, car headlights, cameras and torches all inexplicably failed to work during investigations at the site.

Only a few miles north of Borley lies the Suffolk village of Polstead. There, too, the Rectory is said to be haunted. And when a young Irish vicar moved out after only five nights in his new parish, the church put the 350-year-old building on the market claiming it was "much too large and expensive to maintain."

The Reverend Hayden Foster, 35, arrived in Polstead from Dublin with his wife Margo and son Gerard in April 1978, and for four nights they all slept soundly at their new 16-room home.

On the fifth, the couple moved to another bedroom to accommodate guests who had travelled for Mr Foster's induction ceremony next day. What happened that night was enough to make the family pack their bags in the morning, and move back to Ireland.

Mr Foster told a reporter from the local newspaper, "At about 3 am, we were lying half awake when Margo saw the walls of the room change from being freshly-painted to peeling, damp old wallpaper – just as it might have looked 20 or 30 years ago.

"She heard screaming like a child's, but it wasn't Gerard. Then she felt as if she was being strangled or suffocated. She was trying to say the Lord's Prayer, but she couldn't get it out because of this overwhelming force. I felt too that there was real danger in that room. There is a definite feeling of evil in that place."

Villagers in Polstead were not surprised when the Fosters left. They knew the legends about the Rectory. Some said they had seen a procession of monks crossing the road outside its gates, their sandals six feet above the ground.

Others recalled that the Reverend John Whitmore, vicar from 1795 to 1840, had held an exorcism service in the house.

But the Diocese Bishop, Leslie Brown, had not been told the stories.

He said, "I knew nothing about the Rectory's reputation when the Fosters arrived. If I had, I certainly would never have moved them in.

"The previous vicar had said nothing to me at all, and when I asked his wife about it afterwards, she said, 'Oh well, we got quite used to hearing footsteps going upstairs.'"

A lingering loss

Peter Turner has had more than his fair share of encounters with the supernatural. Some people have seen the same ghost on more than one occasion; but Peter Turner's experiences were years apart and completely unconnected.

The first happened in 1945 when Peter and a group of young friends were playing in a row of derelict houses in the Camp Hill district of Leeds, Yorkshire. The houses were awaiting demolition and provided a natural if dangerous, playground for the local youngsters in austere, post-war Britain.

It was a cold November day and Peter and his friends were playing in a house which had recently had its floorboards removed, leaving only rafters and beams.

As Peter walked across one of the upper-floor rafters he glanced out of the shell of a window. There below him was a neat little garden with an old man tending rose bushes in full bloom.

There was no rubble, no bricks, no broken glass, just a well-kept garden with grass and flowers. The fact that it was impossible for such a garden to exist there at that time, still less contain flowers in full bloom in the middle of winter, didn't occur to young Peter. All he could think about was not getting caught. He and his friends knew what to expect if their parents found out they had been playing in the derelict buildings.

They rushed off, counting their luck at not being spotted by the old man. It was only later that it occurred to Peter how impossible it was for the garden to have been there. He returned to the house but where he had seen roses and flowers there was just brick and rubble.

Eleven years passed and Peter was still living in Leeds and preparing for his wedding, just six months away. Homes were not easy to come by, so Peter and his fiancée Pamela were delighted when they got the top-floor apartment in a Georgian house at 10 Woodhouse Square, previously used as a nursery. One evening Peter and two friends had been decorating the rooms. Feeling hungry, two of them nipped out to get a fish-and-chip supper. On their return they found the third friend outside the flat, too terrified to go back in after hearing strange noises and feeling eerie sensations.

With the excitement of the wedding, the incident was soon forgotten. But no sooner had the newly-married couple moved in, than more strange things began to happen. The door of a large cupboard would swing open, despite being securely fastened. Then footsteps would cross the room and the living room door would swing open.

GHOSTS

When Mrs Turner was working in the kitchen, the cupboard door would swing ajar, there was the sound of shuffling feet and the feeling that someone was standing behind her.

One night, after the Turners had gone to bed, they heard the sound of their settee being dragged across the floor of the living room. When they went to investigate, nothing had been moved.

The sounds continued until one night there was a tremendous crash, just as if the old iron mangle they owned had been thrown on its side. They leapt out of bed and as usual found nothing amiss. But that didn't stop the neighbours in the flat below complaining about the noise the Turners had made "moving their furniture late at night".

The Turners found another home as soon as they could – but not before they discovered a possible cause of the mysterious noises in the night.

By chance, they met an elderly woman who had been brought up in number 10. She remembered, she said, that when she was little, the house was reputedly haunted by a Victorian lady who constantly searched the nursery for her two children who had died there.

Arresting sights

Trainees at the police college at Bramshill, Hampshire are always on the lookout for troublemakers – of the ghostly kind. A "white lady" haunts the galleries of the stately building which now houses the college. Those who have glimpsed her have also caught the definite smell of her lily of the valley perfume.

Another ghostly appearance was reported by a security guard who challenged an unauthorised tennis player. The player instantly vanished through a wall. This ghost is thought to be a nobleman's son who met a tragic end.

A third ghost is reputed to haunt the college. He is known as "the green man" and is said to be a previous occupant of the house who was drowned in the lake in the gardens.

Virginia is now returning to normal

"CHILD HAD NOTHING TO DO WITH POLTERGEIST" — DR NISBET

ELEVEN-YEAR-OLD VIRGINIA CAMPBELL, the Sauchie girl who, it is claimed, is being troubled by a poltergeist, is expected to return to school this week, and there is every indication that her life may soon have returned to normal.

Dr William Nisbet, Tillicoultry, who has been treating Virginia, said at the week-end that the child had nothing to do with the poltergeist which has been plaguing her.

Interviewed at his home, "Hilden," in Stirling Street, Tillicoultry, the doctor said: "Virginia is not responsible for what has happened. The child is innocent.

"What has taken place was not conjured by the child herself, an outside agent is responsible."

Dr Nisbet, father of three children, then added: "Believe me, something unfortunate has been going on in that house.

"I cannot give you an explanation. I have my own thoughts, but they are private for the moment.

"I hope to explain it all fully. But that will be when I have had time to think about it more."

When the poltergeist was first reported, Virginia's mother, Mrs Annie Campbell, called in Dr Nisbet, his partner, Dr William Logan and local minister, Rev. Thomas Lund.

The three have already sent a report to the Church of Scotland.

THE DOG

But last night, Dr Nisbet outlined what he thought was the CAUSE, the EFFECT, and the TREATMENT of the case.

"We have several theories about the cause," he said.

"The most important was the dog that the child left behind in Ireland.

"We thought that this was affecting her mind because it was her pet and she missed it terribly.

"Dr Logan decided to bring his dog to the house to see if its presence would help. It didn't.

"The phenomena went on. It meant that either a dog was not the cause or that her own dog was the only cure.

"The girl was hysterical all the time the phenomena were appearing. We decided then to try sedation."

Dr Nisbet went on: "Virginia was given mild tranquillisers to quieten her.

STILL THERE

"If the phenomena were being conjured by her own imagination they would no longer appear if her brain was dulled."

"But even though the brain was not working normally the phenomena still appeared."

Dr Nisbet paused as his daughter burst into the room, collected some Christmas wrapping and left.

"The next thing we tried was a change of environment.

"Virginia was moved to a house in Dollar for two nights. The manifestations still appeared. She

was brought back to Sauchie and we tried isolation.

"The child was put to bed and left on her own to get to sleep."

"But still the phenomena appeared—and made itself heard. From a room below, we could hear the child screaming and sawing and bouncing noises."

Dr Nisbet continued: "Last Thursday three ministers were sent by the Church of Scotland.

"When Virginia went to bed a short service was held at her bedside. We all prayed."

The doctor paused . . . "Since that night nothing has happened. I believe the cure is now complete.

"In any case, we have on record by cine camera and tape recorder, what has happened — a moving linen box, the lid of the box opening and closing, rippling bedclothes, moving pillows and bouncing noises.

IT'S OVER

"The tape and film will be available to any person who is interested in this case," said Dr Nisbet.

Virginia has been off school for more than a week. But these last three nights she has slept untroubled.

On Sunday the family went for a car drive.

They chatted happily over tea at a wayside cafe. And they reassured each other: "The haunting is over."

Virginia, her cheeks flushed, came dancing into the house after the outing sucking an outsized cat's face lollipop.

She sat giggling at the antics of Popeye on television.

Said her mother: "It's wonderful to see Virginia like her old self again. We want her to forget."

Virginia smiled back at her mother. "I'm happy now," she said.

A cutting from the Alloa Advertiser, Friday, 9th December, 1960.

Answer to an old man's prayer

The young family were happy moving into their new home until the night terror filled their lives. The family, known only as Smith, had started to renovate their 90-year-old wood-frame home in Rochester, New Hampshire. Work had gone well until Mr. Smith tore out an old cast-iron bathtub and put it in another room.

From then on, their lives became hell. That very night came strange sounds and moaning. Said Smith: "I heard footsteps on the stairs and shuffling in the hallway. There was a pounding on the walls and doors slammed shut by themselves." The next night Smith's two daughters were terrorised. The eldest, aged 14, woke up in the night to feel strong gripping hands pushing her by the shoulders into the bed.

She said: "I was terrified. I saw a big, grey-haired man standing in the bathroom doorway. He was wearing a full-length robe, but I couldn't see his features. He just stood there in the doorway – then vanished."

A few nights later, Smith's younger girl, aged two, ran screaming and trembling into her parents room. She huddled in her mother's arms shouting: "Go away, go away. Tell the man to go away."

At first the Smiths thought the girls were having nightmares but the terror returned night after night. They were so scared they slept together in the one room.

In desperation, the family turned to ghost hunter, Norman Gauthier. President of New Hampshire's Society for Psychic Research, Gauthier brought along a priest and a medium.

Both priest and medium agreed there was a ghost in the house, and its spirits came from the bathroom. There, the medium made contact.

"I could see him fully undressed in the tub. He was depressed and lonely. I felt he had a massive brain haemorrhage or a stroke. The old man wanted to know why the Smiths were living in his house and why his bathtub had been removed."

The medium spoke to the spirit and found out that the old man's wife, Althea, had died three years before him.

The medium told him "You are dead. It was a stroke ... calm down. You can see Althea, but you must realise you are dead. You must accept it."

The medium turned to Gauthier and the priest and said: "The old man now knows he is dead and that his wife has gone."

The medium turned to the shaken Smith family. "You won't have any trouble. The old man has left. He has just walked through the door."

Chapter
Three

Horrific Hauntings

Those who believe they have seen a ghost are almost
always upset or disturbed by their eerie experience,
though most later learn to come to terms with it. But
some inexplicable encounters are much more than a
mere fright in the night. These are the horrific
hauntings, the macabre and grisly happenings that
can drive people out of their homes, out of their
minds ... and even cost them their lives.

Horror on a university curriculum

The favourite classes of the curriculum at Camerino University, Italy, were those on the occult, held by a genial professor of psychology, Dr Giuseppi Stoppolini. At one of these classes in September 1950, Stoppolini introduced Maria Bocca to his students. She went into a trance and astounded them all.

In the trance, Maria spoke in the recognisable voices of dead men and women known to those present. But near the end of the seance, came an unfamiliar voice begging them to have mercy and listen.

It said, "I was born Rosa Manichelli. When I died, I was Rosa Spadoni, but my husband has died since then, too. We are both in the cemetery at Castel-Raimondo a few miles from Camerino. I am asking only that you help others, because the same thing can happen to them. Two days after the death certificate was signed, I was taken to the cemetery in a deep coma and buried alive!"

As the students sat in a shocked silence, Maria toppled to the floor in a faint.

The following day, Dr Stoppolini found that there had been a Rosa Spadoni who died in the Civil Hospital in Camerino on September 4, 1939. She was buried two days later at Castel-Raimondo. There were no surviving relatives to protest against exhuming of the body and a small group gathered at Rosa's grave on September 13, 1950.

In addition to Dr Stoppolini and the workmen he had hired, there were pathologists from the Camerino board of health, three officials representing the Italian government and a photographer. An hour of digging uncovered the coffin, and Stoppolini himself stood in the grave to raise the coffin lid.

The skeleton within lay on its back, skull turned to the left. The left arm was bent upward, with the finger bones thrust into the mouth and throat cavity. The knees were bent as if in an effort to force open the lid.

Worse, there were parallel scratches where Rosa had tried to claw her way out of the casket.

The pathologists issued a public statement, which said, "How Dr Stoppolini came by his knowledge is irrelevant. We must agree with him that Rosa Spadoni was buried in a coma when vital signs were undetectable – and that she awakened in her coffin beyond human help."

The Renishaw coffin

Dark secret of the Sitwells

Dame Edith Sitwell

In the Sitwell family it was always known as The Renishaw Coffin. The famous literary trio – Osbert, Edith and Sacheverell – heard about it when they were children and the stories of it and its ghost became part of their upbringing.

Their famous Renishaw Hall, a gloomy Derbyshire mansion dating from 1625, was always thought to be haunted. But it was not until their eccentric father, Sir George Sitwell, decided to improve the house by altering and enlarging the central staircase that the coffin came to light.

In order to carry out the work, two small rooms had to be demolished, one on the ground floor, one a first-floor bedroom. Sir George, who was fanatically proud of his family history, asked the clerk of works to take note of anything interesting he came across, hoping that some traces of ancient building might be found.

65

GHOSTS

The coffin was discovered between the joists of the bedroom floor. From its construction, and the fact that it had nails rather than screws, it was presumed that it dated from the 17th century. It was firmly attached to the joists with iron clamps. Because of lack of space, it had never been fitted with a lid, the floorboards above it serving the purpose. The coffin contained no skeleton, but certain marks proved that there had once been a body in it.

The discovery threw new light on the frightening experiences of two women who had slept in that bedroom when they were guests at Renishaw. The first was a Miss Tait, daughter of Archibald Campbell Tait, the Archbishop of Canterbury. She had been invited to Derbyshire in 1885 to join the house party celebrating Sir George's coming of age.

In the middle of the night she was awakened by someone kissing her three times. The kisses were ice cold. The room was empty.

She ran to the room where Sir George's sister was sleeping and told her what had happened. Miss Sitwell made up a bed for her friend on her sofa, explaining that nothing would induce her to sleep in that room as she had once had exactly the same experience.

After the party, Sir George's agent, Mr Turnbull, came to see him about some business and during the conversation Sir George jokingly told the story of Miss Tait's phantom kisses.

Far from being amused, the agent looked shocked. Apparently, when Sir George had generously lent him Renishaw for his honeymoon, a friend of the agent's bride had come to stay. She had slept in that same bedroom and had had the same experience. She left next morning, obviously frightened, but the Turnbulls had simply credited her with an over-active imagination.

One autumn evening, a few years after Miss Tait's haunting, Lady Sitwell was entertaining a few guests in the upstairs drawing room after dinner. The

---

Lord Brougham's pact

Lord Brougham struck a macabre deal with a fellow student as they discussed life after death one night at Edinburgh University. Whoever died first would re-appear to the other to settle the argument.

The two friends drifted apart after graduating. Brougham's friend went to India, and for years the peer heard nothing from him. But the pact was not forgotten. One day, Brougham stepped from his bath, reached for a towel – and saw his college classmate sitting in a nearby chair.

The peer made a note of the date in his diary: December 19. And in his autobiography, published in 1871, he wrote that shortly afterwards a letter arrived from India. His friend had died.

On December 19.

room was brightly lit and the door stood open onto a passage. She was chatting to a friend who sat on her left when she became conscious of a figure in the passage outside. Friends noticed that she seemed to be following something with her eyes. She wrote later, "I saw the figure with such distinctness that I had no doubt at all that I was looking at a real person."

The figure was that of a woman, apparently a servant, with grey hair done up in a bun under a white cap. Her dress was blue with a full dark skirt. She moved with a furtive, gliding motion as though wishing to escape notice, but her arms were stretched out in front of her and the hands clasped. She moved towards the head of the staircase on which Sir George had worked 20 years before – and disappeared.

Lady Sitwell called out: "Who's that?" When no one answered, she urged her friends to find her the mystery visitor, and everyone joined in the search.

They were on the point of giving up when a young woman, looking down into the well-lit hall below, suddenly cried out, "I do believe that's the ghost!"

Just where the door of the old room used to be, she saw a woman with dark hair and dress obviously distressed and in deep thought. Her figure, though opaque, cast no shadow. It moved in a gentle glide, full of sadness, and melted away. What happened in the two rooms that Sir George demolished has never been discovered and the empty coffin has kept its secret.

Stroll to oblivion

David Lang vanished from the face of the earth on September 23, 1880, and, has never been heard of since – apart from his ghostly voice. His disappearance, on a sunny afternoon and in front of five witnesses, remains one of the most baffling mysteries of all time.

During his last moments, Lang, a prosperous farmer, was strolling across a field in front of his home near Gallatin, Tennessee. His children, George, eight, and Sarah, 11, were playing in the front of the house. His wife had just walked out of the house to greet an approaching buggy carrying Judge August Peck and his brother-in-law.

David smiled, waved at the visitors and started walking toward the group at the farmhouse. He took a dozen steps, then Mrs Lang's horrified scream shattered the afternoon. Judge Peck dropped the buggy reins. The two men sprinted across the field to join Mrs Lang and the children at the spot where

Ripper's legacy

Two victims of Jack the Ripper have returned to London's East End to remind the capital city of its most celebrated unsolved crimes.

Polly Nicholls, a 42-year-old prostitute, was the first of the cruel butcher's six victims, found with her throat and stomach cut on August 31, 1888. She had been seen since, a huddled, pathetic figure, glowing eerily in the gutter of Durward Street, Whitechapel, where her body was discovered.

Harrowing screams heard in Hansbury Street, in nearby Spitalfields, are said to be those of another of Jack's victims, 47-year-old Annie Chapman.

David Lang had last been seen.

There was no trace of the farmer. In full view of five witnesses, he had simply vanished.

His wife fell to her knees and began to beat frantically at the ground. Judge Peck lifted her to her feet and the five fanned out in a frantic search of the pasture. The search yielded no sign of the missing man.

The judge summoned help. Neighbours began to arrive and search parties were formed. Far into the night, lanterns were swinging across the farm and through the woods beyond.

The next morning the county surveyor arrived and inspected the area where Lang had vanished. He announced that it was firmly supported by thick strata of limestone. There were no potholes or caves into which a man could fall.

Mrs Lang was by now numb with shock and under her doctor's care. As the search continued through days, weeks and eventually months, she stoutly resisted any suggestion of a funeral or even a memorial service for David Lang. She asked only that all churches pray for his return.

The shock of the experience had deeply affected the two Lang children – particularly Sarah. She turned into a shy, withdrawn child who spent long hours day-dreaming. Finally there was an astounding incident that prompted Mrs Lang to take her children away from the farm.

On an April evening in 1881, Sarah ran sobbing into the house to report that there was a "ring" around the spot where her father had vanished. When Mrs Lang went to investigate, the child said she could clearly hear her father calling. He was begging for help in a tortured voice, but it faded away into silence.

Mrs Lang did not hear her husband's ghostly voice, but in the pasture she made a strange discovery. Where her husband had last been seen, there was a perfect circle of withered yellow grass some 20 feet in diameter.

The race to eternity

A never-ending marathon

The day "marathon man" James Worson accepted a sporting challenge was the day he disappeared from the face of the earth. The proud, athletic, English shoemaker screamed once, and vanished forever.

On September 3, 1873, Worson boasted of his athletic prowess to two fellow townsfolk of Leamington, Warwickshire. He said that on more than one occasion he had raced from one town to another in record time.

The people of Leamington knew Worson's talents as a footracer, but his friends were sceptical. He might be as good as he thought, they told him, but could he prove it? Worson happily accepted the challenge. He would show them, he said, with a 20-mile run from Leamington to Coventry.

They began the test in high spirits. Worson put on his running clothes and set out. His friends, Hammerson Burns and Barham Wise, trailed close behind him in a horse-drawn gig, Burns carrying a camera.

The mood of the three was still festive a quarter of the way to Coventry. Worson appeared as tireless as he had claimed, running with ease and turning occasionally to exchange words with his friends.

The runner was never out of their sight. Running in the middle of the dirt road, Worson suddenly appeared to stumble. He pitched forward in a headlong fall and had time for only one piercing scream. Wise said later, "It was the most ghastly sound either of us had ever heard."

That terrible cry was their last memory of him. Worson's body never struck the ground – he vanished in the middle of his fall without touching the earth.

The road itself provided tangible evidence of what they had witnessed. Burns' pictures of the long-distance runner's tracks – clear footprints in the soft dirt, faltering and ending as abruptly as if Worson had crashed into a stone wall.

When the men returned to Leamington a massive hunt began. Searchers combed every inch of the terrain between Leamington and Coventry without success. Bloodhounds were strangely reluctant to approach the spot where Worson's footprints ended. And for years after his disappearance there were reports of a ghostly green runner on the empty night road from Leamington to Coventry.

Hands of grisly glory

Thieves in the 18th century tried to ensure success for their crimes by invoking the aid of the dead.

The villains believed a candle gripped in the cut-off hand of a man who died on the gallows had the supernatural power to stupefy anyone they wished to rob.

In the 1790s, a traveller in woman's clothing arrived at the Old Spital Inn, which stood at Stainmore between Barnard Castle and Brough on windswept Bowes Moor in County Durham. The new arrival asked only to be allowed to doze by the fire before continuing her journey.

The landlord ordered a maid to sit with the visitor. The maid was suspicious, for she was sure she had spotted trousers peeping below the skirts of the "woman". The maid pretended to be asleep. When all was quiet, the traveller pulled out a hand taken from the body of an executed felon, and wedged a candle between the dead fingers. He recited: "Let those who sleep, sleep on, let those who are awake be awake." The man then unlocked the door and called softly to accomplices waiting outside.

The watchful maid wasted no time. She rushed at the door, slamming it shut and bolting it, with the would-be raiders outside. She then dashed upstairs to rouse her employer, but she could not waken him. Downstairs the door was being smashed by the gang.

The candle was still burning in its macabre holder, and the girl remembered the legend that only extinguishing the flame with milk broke its spell.

She grabbed a jug of skimmed milk from the kitchen and upended it over

---

The dragoon's hand

The ghostly hand of Trumpet Major Blandford haunts the Dorset village of Tarrant Hinton. Blandford was a member of the British Army's famed dragoons, but he enjoyed a spot of poaching in his spare time.

He and some other men were illegally stalking deer in the grounds of Cranborne Chase on December 16, 1780, when they were surprised by gamekeepers. Several men were wounded, and one of the keepers later died during a bitter gun battle across Chettle Common.

Blandford lost his hand but escaped to London, where he died. The severed hand was buried in the Dorset churchyard of Pimperne – and locals say it sometimes appears in search of the arm to which it was once attached.

the hand. The flame died – and as it did so, the landlord and his staff were woken by the noise downstairs. The thieves promised to leave once their candle was returned, but they were forced to flee empty-handed when the innkeeper opened fire with his shotgun.

The grisly candle-holders were called Hands of Glory, and similar stories have been heard in other parts of England, and in France, Belgium and Ireland.

One encyclopedia of superstition lists the mysterious ingredients of the candle as the fat of a hanged man, virgin wax and Lapland sesame.

Mystery of the planter's tomb

The riddle of the Barbados coffins is one of the most baffling supernatural mysteries of all time. For 12 years, unseen forces repeatedly desecrated a sealed tomb on the Caribbean island. Eventually the family which owned the crypt was forced to abandon it. Only then did the bodies of their departed rest in peace.

The Chase family, slave-owning sugar planters, acquired the tomb in 1808. It was built of stone, recessed into the cliffs above Oistin's Bay, and sealed with a marble slab. When the family took it over, it already held one wooden coffin, that of a Mrs Thomasina Goddard.

Twice within a year, the slab guarding the only entrance was rolled aside as the family buried two of their children, Mary Ann and Dorcas. In 1812, their father Thomas also died. Eight men carried the lead coffin up to the headland, but when the tomb was opened, the mourners gasped in horror.

Mrs Goddard's body still lay in its proper place, but the caskets containing the children were standing on end against one of the walls. There was no sign of a break-in.

Pallbearers gently restored the two tiny coffins to their positions, then lugged in the box containing Mr Chase. It was laid beside the others. Stonemasons carefully cemented the marble slab securely across the entrance.

Four years later, they returned to bury a boy relative, and found the seals were intact. But again there was torment for the tragic family. The same sight of desecration met their grieving gaze when the slab was removed.

Order was restored, with eight men struggling to lift Mr Chase's coffin back to its place, but by now, the tomb was the talking point of the entire

71

island. Two months later, new coffins were added – and the same chaos was discovered. And the same happened in 1819 when the next burial took place.

Each time, Mrs Goddard's casket was undisturbed, which seemed to rule out flooding or earth tremors. The stone walls and ceilings were checked, but no faults found. There was only one way in, and each time the cement seals around the slab were unbroken. Fear of sacred places ruled out interference by the islanders, even if it had been physically possible.

Lord Combermere, Governor of Barbados, was among the stunned funeral party in 1819. As the family wept, he personally supervised the orderly arrangement of the coffins, which now totalled six, and sprinkled fine sand around them. When the entrance slab was again cemented in place, he added his seal to the joint.

On April 18 the following year, he unexpectedly asked the rector of the nearby church to open the tomb. The six coffins which had been laid in a neat line, the three smaller ones resting on top of those containing adults. Now they were again scattered around the cave.

Mr Chase's casket was once more standing upright, with only Mrs Goddard lying where she had been left. There were no marks in the sand, and Lord Combermere's seal was intact.

The Chases could no longer stand the notoriety the tomb was bringing them. All their family coffins were carried to Christ Church graveyard, and buried in a joint funeral ceremony.

Sir Arthur Conan Doyle, creator of Sherlock Holmes and an avid investigator of the paranormal, took an interest in the story. He put forward the theory that supernatural forces played havoc with the coffins because they were made of lead, and so delayed the decomposition of the bodies. He also believed that Thomas Chase committed suicide.

But for all his theorising, the abandoned tomb has kept its secret and may do so forever.

Judge who hanged his daughter

A judge who sentenced his own daughter to death has haunted Kilworthy House, at Tavistock, Devon, for nearly 400 years.

Judge John Glanville broke the heart of his daughter, Elizabeth, when he forbade her to marry the man she loved, a naval lieutenant. Instead he forced her to become the bride of a man considered more worthy of her, a Plymouth goldsmith.

Elizabeth, her maid and the sailor murdered the husband, but were arrested within days. Judge Glanville sent all three to the gallows – and his penitent ghost has been suffering for it ever since.

The menace of Berkeley Square

London's elegant Berkeley Square is today as calm and peaceful as any
such place in the middle of a bustling capital can be.

Office workers spend the summer lunchtimes relaxing on its lawns,
while after dark gamblers and revellers flock to its clubs and casinos. And
traffic speeding through this fashionable area of Mayfair makes it hard for
tourists to hear the nightingale immortalised in a wartime hit song.

But less than a century ago, Berkeley Square was the most feared place in
Britain. For the house at No 50, today a bookshop, was the home of the
deadliest spectral killer of all time. Even now, no one is sure exactly what
caused the deaths that alarmed Victorian England, for few who saw the killer
lived to tell the tale. Those who survived generally became incoherent with
sheer terror.

The house was already the talk of the town when Sir Robert Warboys
accepted a foolhardy challenge at his club, White's. The handsome
adventurer scoffed when friends discussed the possible causes of the disasters
at No 50, and vowed to spend a night there to prove that talk of supernatural
happenings was nonsense.

The owner of the house, a man called Benson, was reluctant to allow the
experiment, but Sir Robert would not be dissuaded. He agreed, under
pressure, to take a gun with him. And Benson insisted that Sir Robert's
friends and himself stand guard on the floor below the bedroom where he
would spend the night. If anything strange happened, the young aristocrat
was to pull a cord which rang a bell in a room on the first floor.

Sir Robert retired at 11.15 pm after a good dinner. Just 45 minutes later,
the bell began to jangle. As the rescue party raced upstairs, they heard a
shot. They burst into the room to find Sir Robert slumped across the bed, his
head dangling over the side.

He was dead – but not from a bullet wound. His eyes bulged in terror, his
lips were curled hideously above clenched teeth. He had died of fright.

Intrigued by this and other stories about the deadly house in Berkeley
Square, Lord Lyttleton resolved to investigate the mystery and arranged to
spend a night in the room where Sir Robert had died.

He took along two guns, one filled with shot, the other with silver sixpenny
pieces – charms to ward off evil spirits. During the night, he fired the barrel
of coins at a shape that leapt at him. In 1879, he published the full details of

---

Spectral squatter

A couple were given a house by their local council because they said their old home was haunted. James and Julie Mentiply claimed to have been terrified by the ghost of the previous tenant, an old lady who died of a heart attack.

After seeing it just once, 22-year-old Mrs Mentiply, ran out of the house in Stone, Buckinghamshire, and refused to go back.

---

the ordeal in his book, *Notes and Queries*. He concluded that the room was "supernaturally fatal to body and mind".

Lyttleton's researches included the discovery that a girl who had stayed at the house as a guest had been driven mad by terror. A man who had slept one night in the haunted room had been found dead next morning. And the maid of a family renting the place had died in hospital after being found crumpled on the floor whimpering, "Don't let it touch me."

Not surprisingly, few people were anxious to move into the house. For years it stood empty, its paintwork peeling, its secret undisturbed. Then, in December 1887, the frigate *Penelope* docked in Portsmouth, and its crew went ashore to head for home.

Two sailors, Edward Blunden and Robert Martin, arrived in London on Christmas Eve with little money and no lodgings for the night. They wandered the streets for a while before finding themselves in Berkeley Square. They soon discovered the To Let signs outside No 50. There was no doubt that the house was vacant and the men decided to spend the night there.

They wandered through the neglected rooms, arriving at last in a second-floor bedroom which seemed in better order than the others. Martin was soon asleep but his shipmate was nervous. As he tossed and turned, Blunden heard strange footsteps scratching along the corridor outside their door. He woke Martin, and the two watched, hearts racing, as the door slowly opened and something large, dark and shapeless entered the room.

Blunden darted towards the fireplace to try to grab something he could use as a weapon. As the intruder went after the terrified sailor, Martin seized the chance to escape through the open door. He raced down the stairs and ran for help. In nearby Piccadilly, he blurted his story to a police constable and the two men hurried back to the house.

They were too late. The shattered body of Blunden, his neck broken, his face fixed in a grimace of unimaginable terror, was sprawled on the basement steps.

Screaming skull
A skull is kept at Bettiscombe Manor, Dorset. Whenever it is taken out of doors it is said to scream. And when the outbreak of war is near, the skull is said to perspire blood.

The hell hounds

Dogs, cats and horses have always been associated with the spirit world. They are said to sense, even see, ghosts which are invisible to the human eye. But some animals exist as four-legged phantoms themselves. The most terrifying are the giant black hounds of hell.

Almost every part of Britain has such legends: fiendish harbingers of doom with blazing eyes and snarling teeth. The Yorkshire version, the Padfoot, is said to be as big as a donkey. The Welsh call theirs Gwyllgi, and the Lancashire dog is known as Trash or Shriker. On the Isle of Man, the Mauthe or Moddey Dhoo is said to haunt Peel Castle, and soldiers once refused to patrol the battlements there alone.

One sentry who dared to serve solo was found gibbering next morning, and died three days later.

The most frequently documented hell hound is Black Shuck, whose name is derived from Scucca, the Saxon word for the Devil. Hundreds of people claim to have seen him at night in the lonely fenlands of East Anglia, the one eye in the centre of his head blazing scarlet or yellow.

He has been reported on the coast near Cromer, loping along lanes near the Norfolk Broads at Neatishead, and at Wicken Fen, near Newmarket. In Suffolk, people living near the heathland of Walberswick and Dunwich call him the Galley Trot. And it was in this area, during World War Two, that he gave an American airman and his wife a night they would never forget.

The couple had rented a flat-topped hut on the edge of Walberswick Marsh while the husband served at a nearby air base. One stormy evening they were startled by a violent pounding on the door. The airman peeped through a window and saw a huge black beast battering their home.

The terrified couple piled what little furniture they had against the door, then cowered as the attacker hurled his body against first one wall, then another, then leapt on to the roof. The ordeal lasted several hours before the noise faded away. The couple waited anxiously for daylight, and at dawn crept outside to inspect the damage. There was no sign of the attack, and no paw or claw marks in the soft mud around the hut.

The West Country is said to have a pack of wild black dogs, whose blood-curdling howls have been heard several times across the vast wastes of Dartmoor.

But a different phantom beast worried hundreds of people in five Devon towns when they woke one winter's morning in February, 1855. Clearly visible in the heavy overnight snow were animal footprints four inches long and almost three inches wide – footprints which, it was later discovered, stretched in a zig-zag trail for nearly 100 miles from Totnes to Littleham. Dogs brought in to track the mystery creature through undergrowth at Dawlish backed off, howling dismally. Baffled investigators found that at one stage, the trail went into a shed through a six-inch hole. In another place, the prints indicated that the animal had squeezed through a long narrow drainpipe. Next night, local people bolted their doors and refused to venture outside. They were convinced the Devil himself had walked through Devon.

Journalist and ghost-collector W T Stead told of a letter sent to him in 1902 by an Englishman who went hunting in the South African Transvaal. The man claimed he was riding back to camp when an eerie white horse carrying an unearthly rider emerged from a thicket of trees, and pursued him. That night, one of the hunter's guides told him of an earlier safari, when an Englishman shot seven elephants in the thicket. He returned next morning to collect the ivory tusks – and was never seen again. His white horse returned to camp alone, but died 24 hours later. The guide added, "I would not go into that bush for all the ivory in the land."

Petrified poacher

Poacher Jim Mace never lived to tell the tale of his midnight meeting with a beautiful woman. But his voice is still heard, just one of the unearthly sounds that make Breckles Hall one of Norfolk's most mysterious stately homes.

Mace and another man decided to go shooting partridge in the hall grounds one night early this century after drinking in a local inn. They knew the legends about the place. Screams for mercy, banging doors and strange footsteps had been heard, and on rare occasions the ballroom shimmered with the glow of spectral dancers. After bagging their birds, the intrepid hunters crept up to the hall in search of ghosts.

At first they were disappointed, for the windows of the empty mansion stayed dark. Only the wind disturbed the still of the night. The two men turned for home, then stopped in their tracks. A coach pulled by four horses swept silently into sight at the bottom of the drive, heading for the house. Rooted to the ground by fear, the men gazed as it came to a halt in front of the main doors, and a beautiful, bejewelled woman stepped out. She stared straight into Mace's eyes – and he slumped to the ground with a piercing shriek.

The sound seemed to break the spell which held his friend motionless. He raced to the nearest house to get help. But he could find no one prepared to go near the hall until daylight.

Next morning the vicar led a posse of villagers to the spot. The body of the poacher lay stiff and cold, his face a mask of terror.

Beware of the bones

The dead keep a vengeful watch

People who tamper with the remains of the dead, or ignore the last wishes of the dying do so at their peril. It seems that the spirits of the departed keep a careful watch on their earthly relics, and are quick to intervene if anything untoward happens to them.

An American farmer called Walsingham was exploring his new home at Oakville, Georgia, when he came across an ancient skeleton and threw it into a lime kiln. Soon doors began to slam in the middle of the night, chairs were mysteriously overturned, and bells tolled through the rooms.

Walsingham was not a superstitious man. He put the curious sounds down to mischief by neighbours. Then a series of things happened which he could not ignore. They were described by the *San Francisco Examiner* in 1891.

First the man's dog began barking furiously at a wall. One day the animal lunged towards it and fell back yelping, its neck broken as if somebody had hurled its body backwards.

Hideous laughter, shouts and wails began coming from all over the house. One of Walsingham's daughters saw a disembodied hand grasp her shoulder. And the farmer watched aghast as the prints of a naked pair of feet formed beside him as he walked in the rain.

The last straw for the family came at a dinner party. Guests shrugged off strange groans from the room above. Then a red stain began to form on the white tablecloth, spreading as more scarlet drips fell from the ceiling.

The men in the party raced upstairs and began tearing up the floorboards. But they found only dry dust, even though the liquid – later identified by chemical tests as human blood – continued to spread on the table. The Walsinghams packed their belongings and moved out of the haunted home.

A skull called Awd Nance has caused headaches for successive occupants of Burton Agnes Hall, a beautiful English mansion in a village between Bridlington and Driffield in Yorkshire. For more than 300 years the gruesome relic has insisted on staying in the house. Those who have tried to get rid of it have been forced to think again.

The hall was built by three spinster sisters early in the 17th century, financed by a legacy from their father, Sir Henry Griffith. Soon after the building was completed, robbers ambushed the youngest sister, Anne, as she returned from visiting friends in nearby Harpham. Villagers gently carried her battered body home. She was well cared for, but her injuries were so severe that it was clear she would never recover.

Shortly before she died, Anne made an extraordinary request. She insisted that her sisters cut off her head before they buried her body, and preserve it in the walls of her beloved home. She threatened that if they did not do so, dire consequences would follow. The two sisters promised they would follow her wishes, but the idea horrified them. When Anne died, they buried her body intact.

Seven days later, an inexplicable crash in an upstairs room woke the whole household. After another week, the family were again roused from their sleep when doors slammed in every part of the building. Three weeks after the funeral, they lay terrified in their beds all night as the whole house shook with the clatter of crowds of invisible beings running along corridors and up and down stairs. Agonised groans echoed through the rooms.

Next morning the servants quit. The sisters called in the local vicar, and when they mentioned Anne's dying wish, he agreed to open the grave. The body was just as they had last seen it – except for the head. That had been cut off, and all the skin had shrivelled away, leaving the skull bare.

Reluctantly, the sisters carried the grim memento into the hall. The haunting ceased. The skull stayed with them for the rest of their lives.

Several subsequent owners of Burton Agnes have dared to throw out Awd Nance, but each time, mysterious shuffling and scratching sounds, slamming doors and terrifying groans have forced them to restore the relic to its rightful place.

Other ghosts have been responsible for the finding of human bones in places where they should not have been. Such spectres vanish only once the bones have been given a decent burial.

Guests at a house in Lynton, Devon, complained during the 1930s that

---

Vigilante tragedy

A white phantom caused a bizarre tragedy in Hammersmith, London, in 1804. Vigilante patrols were set up after the ghost chased and seized a woman as she walked through a graveyard. She died from shock a few days later. Sixteen people travelling past the church on a horse-drawn cart also fled the eerie shape.

On the fourth night of the vigil, one of the volunteers, customs officer Francis Smith, spotted a figure in white moving down a nearby lane. He shot at it, and the figure fell. But it was not a ghost. It was bricklayer Thomas Milwood, coming home late from work in his white overalls. Smith was tried for manslaughter, and sentenced to death but, on appeal, the sentence was reduced to a year in prison.

GHOSTS

Voices from the grave

Friedrich Jurgenson's tape-recorder plays back voices of the dead. Jurgenson, a Stockholm artist, says he has no idea how the voices get on his tapes. Yet over several years his machine has picked up more than 140 voices, including those of Adolf Hitler and Death Row's Caryl Chessman.

Hitler's voice was the first to appear on Jurgenson's tape in 1960. He had recorded a memorandum and, when playing back his notes, heard other voices. He had the machine tested, but nothing was wrong with it. Yet when he made a further tape and played it back, his voice was drowned out.

This time the sounds were voices saying: "We live, we live. We are not dead." A German engineer listened to the tape and identified the voice as Hitler's. The voice seemed to be apologising for concentration camp atrocities. The voice was compared with recordings of Hitler and was again identified as the voice of the Nazi leader.

---

they could never get a decent night's sleep in the room above the skullery. They told their hosts, the Ewing family, that they saw the ghost of an old woman, and heard the sobbing of a child.

Then Mrs Ewing's brother-in-law realised that the haunted bedroom was much narrower than the skullery below it. The family discovered a cupboard which had been walled up. Inside was a child's box, and a collection of ancient human bones. Only when they were removed did peace reign in the house.

Frederick Fisher was a poor Australian farmer whose profits from crops never covered the cost of his living. Eventually he was taken to court, and jailed for debt. To stop creditors seizing his farm at Cambelltown, New South Wales, he transferred it to the name of an associate called George Worrall.

Six months later, Fisher finished his sentence and returned to his home. But one night in 1826 he left a nearby inn after a heavy drinking session – and was never seen again. Police investigated the disappearance, but could find no evidence of foul play.

Months went by. Then came the dark night that neighbour James Farley got the shock of his life. A strange figure was sitting on one of his fences, pointing to a spot in Fisher's paddock. Farley was too scared to do anything until daylight. Next morning he guided a police constable to the site the phantom had indicated, and in the shallow grave, discovered the badly beaten body of farmer Fisher.

George Worrall was questioned, and found to be an ex-convict. He confessed and was hanged. His victim's ghost was never seen again.

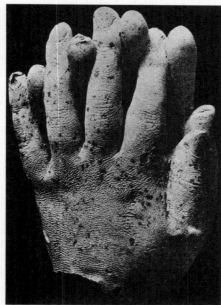

The Polish medium Franek Kluski worked in Warsaw and the materialisation above took place on 25 December 1919. On the left is a pair of wax hands made in Kluski's presence by a pair of hands that had materialised. The materialised hands made an impression of themselves in the wax.

The Tennessee demon

The terror that sent John Bell to his grave started in 1817. At first there were just scratching noises at doors and windows, as though someone – or something – was trying to get into his remote farmhouse home in Robertson County, Tennessee.

Farmer John would look outside, but there was nothing to be seen. It was worrying, even frightening, but he was able to reassure his wife and children ... until the night whatever had been trying to enter his house succeeded.

Frightening sounds filled the rooms – the rush of wings, a ratlike gnawing, the muffled pad of animal paws. As days passed, the noises grew louder and stronger, as if whatever was causing them was growing in power. The raps became solid crashes and there were muffled gasps and gurgles as of someone trying to talk.

In the upstairs room where she slept alone, 13-year-old Betsy Bell awoke one night screaming. An invisible force was pinching and slapping her. There were similar attacks on the other children and they steadily grew in ferocity.

The terrified family, all well-liked churchgoers, tried to keep their horror a secret – although friends noticed John Bell was looking sick and haunted.

Finally, they could stand it no longer and invited a neighbour, James Johnson, to their home and told him the horrid story. Johnson, a lay preacher, listened and tried to exorcise the demon.

Despite his hymns and prayers, the attempt failed and the angered demon slapped poor Betsy, knocking the screaming girl to the floor.

The family begged John to take them away from the house, but he refused. He said the demon was his "cross to bear" and refused to budge.

The demon grew stronger. The gurgle turned to a husky, rasping whisper that would coo and curse, recited whole chapters from the Bible, and then lapse into obscene blasphemies.

The demon's words were, for the most part, a frightful gibberish – but each message carried the same theme. It hated John Bell and swore it would hound him to the grave.

Fear now spread through the county, and the family's once loyal friends began to shun them. Some believed that young Betsy was the witch. Old John's mind and body finally broke under the terrible assault and he suffered frequent convulsions.

A doctor had prescribed medicine for the old man, and during one attack his son went to get it. Instead of the doctor's medicine, he found the bottle filled with a murky fluid.

The family sent for the doctor and, while they waited, the demon rampaged triumphantly through the house. Its whisper was a hoarse grunt: "I've got him this time! I gave him a big dose while he was sleeping and Old Jack is done for now!"

John Bell died on December 20, 1820. The doctor tested the potion on a cat – and it died.

He told the inquest, "All the time, I could hear that cursed thing laughing and gloating. Oh, I know some people hint that Betsy had been throwing her voice, and I thought it was possible too. But when I clapped my hand across her mouth, the voice kept sniggering and talking."

After the funeral, the demon told the family it would return in seven years. Right on time, it again visited the family, but both the son, John junior, and Betsy were happily married. Disappointed, the demon said it would return in 107 years.

The threat was never carried out and 1935 passed safely for John's heir Dr Charles Bell.

Lesson of death

Twelve schoolboys were shocked to see their classmate John Daniel sitting at his desk. For seven weeks earlier John had been found dead 200 yards from his home in Beaminster, Dorset. His death had been recorded as "from natural causes" after his mother said he suffered from fits.

After questioning the 12 boys, local magistrate Colonel Broadrep, ordered the body to be exhumed, and an inquest in 1728 revealed that John had been strangled. The murderer was never caught.

John's ghost never returned to his old school, but his pathetic figure has been seen in nearby St Mary's Church.

Gisele's burning memories

From the moment he saw the old house, Paul Fortier knew it would be an appropriate setting for the good years ahead. That they were going to be good years, he had no doubt.

His first novel, *Fields of Amaranth*, was doing well, and he was at work on a second that promised to be even better. What was more, he had a beautiful

Brush with a ghost

Vicar's daughter Elsie Marshall was just 21 years old in 1893 when she was murdered by bandits in China where she worked as a missionary. She is believed to be the invisible being which brushes past staff of the library which now occupies her former home in Blackheath, London.

young wife and a five-year-old daughter who was the image of her mother.

Denise Fortier also liked the house in Montreal, Canada – but with reservations. After they bought it in 1905, she began to wish that Paul had looked into its history as carefully as he had checked the foundations.

From neighbours she was to learn that the house had been involved in some of Montreal's most blood-chilling crimes.

Built in 1805 as a detention home for "wayward children", it was wrecked by fire after two of the children had murdered the owner and his wife. In spite of their age, the children were hanged.

The house was rebuilt, but for more than a century was plagued by disasters. They included arson, murder, and inexplicable double suicides. And there were "cold spots" – pockets of numbingly cold air that seemed to move from room to room.

Denise became increasingly apprehensive about their new home, and Paul began to look at her with growing doubt and pity. In desperation, Denise went to her priest. Though the good man listened sympathetically as she urged him to exorcise the house, she thought that his face mirrored some of Paul's scepticism. Denise went home that evening with the certainty that something frightful was going to happen.

Looking at her husband that evening, she was sure that Paul had changed. He drank too much wine at the dinner table and became morose. Something in their mood seemed to communicate itself to five-year-old daughter Gisele. Sensing that the little girl was frightened, Denise carried her off to bed.

The child whispered, "Can we leave here sometime soon?"

"I don't know, dear. Why?"

"Those cold spots you tried to show daddy – I think there was one in my bed last night. I woke up with my teeth chattering even though the room was hot."

Trying to conceal her own fear, Denise bent and kissed her. "It was probably just a bad dream," she said.

They were the last words the little girl heard from her mother's lips.

That night the child again woke to a nightmare. It began with a suffocating odour of smoke in the house. Screaming, she ran to her parents' bedroom and flung open the door. The walls and ceiling of the room were ablaze, but there were infinitely worse horrors.

Her father's body lay close to the bed with a pair of scissors driven into his throat. And in the deep, soft bed her mother was struggling with two naked boys scarcely bigger than Gisele. Denise's lips yawned in a silent scream as the giggling children pummelled her body.

But when Gisele returned from next door with help, the room had changed so inexplicably that the little girl's story would always be doubted.

There was no fire in the room, and no evidence that there had been one. The vicious children had vanished. Beaten almost beyond recognition, there was only her mother's unconscious body and the corpse of Paul Fortier.

Police concluded that Gisele's story was pure fantasy subconsciously devised to conceal the facts. Obviously there had been a savage family quarrel in which she had seen her battered mother kill her father in self-defence.

It was a theory Denise herself could neither confirm nor deny. In a catatonic state, she was taken to a hospital where she died three months later. The orphaned child went to live with her grandparents in Seattle.

Because of fear of its ghostly inhabitants, the Fortier house was never again occupied. It burned to the ground in 1906.

Date with doom

Lord Thomas Lyttleton was in surprisingly jovial mood as he sat down to breakfast with close friends at his home in Epsom, Surrey, on November 24, 1779. But his guests choked on their kidneys and kedgeree as he joked that he had been visited during the night by the ghost of a girl who had killed herself after he seduced and deserted her.

She said that in exactly three days he would be dead.

Later that day, the peer made a magnificent speech in the House of Lords. He continued his roistering life as one of the great characters of London society. He assured friends he had never felt better, and arranged to stay the following weekend with Peter Andrews, a Member of Parliament who lived in Dartford, Kent.

But on the third night, as the clock struck the eleventh hour, Lyttleton suddenly clutched at his side, collapsed and died in the arms of his valet.

At exactly that moment, Andrews woke at Dartford to find the peer standing beside his bed, wearing the dressing gown the MP had left out for him.

"It's all over with me, Andrews," said the figure. Andrews followed his friend, but found Lyttleton's room empty, the dressing gown still hanging on its hook. Next morning he learned of his friends death.

A Rover's return

Cecil Bathe had just driven past a wrecked German tank during World War Two when a sandstorm struck. The Royal Air Force mechanic, returning to his Libyan base after a supply trip, decided to wait it out. He sat reading a dog-eared magazine and drinking beer given to him earlier by some Australian pals.

As a gust of wind shook his three-ton truck, Cecil looked up, and saw a lone uniformed figure in the whirling dust. He beckoned the man to the lorry and told him to jump in. Both sheltered from the lashing sand outside, chatting and swigging beer.

The stranger, wearing a khaki uniform without any insignia, spoke in a clipped, rather stilted accent. But after two years of desert warfare, Cecil paid no heed to the rather ragged look, and put the accent down to either South African or Dutch, both fighting alongside the Allies.

As they drank, the Englishman noticed his stranded companion had a raw burn on his right hand and arm. He urged the stranger to get medical attention, but the only response was a chilling laugh and the words, "It's a bit late for that. Anyway, it doesn't matter."

But Cecil did discover that he and his eerie companion had something in common. Before the war both had been Rover Scouts and had attended an international jamboree in southern England.

A toast to tragedy

The Fleur de Lys pub at the Somerset village of Norton St Philip, is haunted by a man who stopped there for a drink 300 years ago – and paid for it with his life.

Rebels who had supported the Duke of Monmouth's uprising were being tried in a court across the road, at what is now the George Inn, and those sentenced to die were led to their execution in an orchard behind the Fleur de Lys, via a passage beside the bar.

The thirsty traveller held open a gate for one party of condemned men, but was hustled on with them by guards, and hanged in error.

William Harris, who became landlord of the Fleur de Lys in 1974, heard jangling chains in the icy cold passage, and his wife saw a shadowy figure walk up the corridor of the empty pub.

The previous landlord once locked his dog in the office for an hour while he went out. On his return, the animal was out of its mind with terror, bolted into the road and was run over.

Daylight had begun to fade as the wind dropped and the RAF man decided to try to make a run for his camp. He offered the stranger a lift, but he shook his head. "I'm going in the other direction," he said. "Thank you for the beer."

The man stepped down from the truck and they shook hands. "God watch over you, Tommy," said the stranger. Cecil felt that the hand he was shaking was cold and stiff.

Cecil drove away, but there was no trace of the uniformed figure in the rearview mirror. He got out to look, but all he could see was the wrecked shell of the enemy tank.

Later that week Cecil returned to the airfield by motorbike just as a recovery crew was hauling the tank wreck onto a transporter.

He stopped to look and the corporal in charge told him that the tank driver had died at the controls a month before when the tank was hit in the turret by a shell. They had laid the body out under canvas.

Cecil lifted the makeshift shroud.

There, with decaying skin and dead eyes, was his beer-drinking desert companion of a few days earlier.

Shaken, Cecil dropped the groundsheet. He clambered onto the tank wreck and peered into the half-light. Glinting in the sunlight he could see an Australian beer bottle.

Chapter Four

Ghosts of the Deep

For centuries, seafarers have returned to port to tell salty tales of life on the ocean waves. Their fireside stories of daring deeds, strange countries and weird monsters enthralled generations of land-lubbers. Today, we know that many of the tales were pure fantasy. But we also know that some stories of baffling events are factual; that when it comes to ghosts, past and present, stranger things really have happened at sea ...

Unexpected guest for tea

A tea party was taking place at the home of Vice-Admiral Sir George and Lady Tryon in London's fashionable Eaton Square. The mansion was crowded with the cream of the capital's society. Sir George, in full dress uniform, walked down the graceful curved staircase towards his guests. Lady Tryon dropped her teacup and screamed.

The guests watched aghast as the famous admiral reached the foot of the stairs, calmly and silently crossed the room, opened a door and was gone. It was June 22, 1893, and the guests knew that they had just seen a ghost. For that day Sir George was on the bridge of his flagship, *Victoria*, off Tripoli and, tragically, was guiding her into one of Britain's greatest naval disasters.

His squadron steamed along in two columns as part of a carefully planned fleet exercise. *Victoria* led one of the columns, with the *Camperdown* heading the other.

The naval squadron consisted of Britain's entire Mediterranean Fleet – eight ironclad battleships and five cruisers. Sir George's plan called for the two columns to move within six cable lengths of each other. Steaming ahead on parallel courses, they would turn inward on command and then reverse course. But were six cable lengths – about 4,500 feet – enough?

One officer meekly suggested that the two columns could come dangerously close to a collision.

The Vice-Admiral agreed that perhaps there should be eight cable lengths. However, within minutes he again mysteriously changed his mind, ordering the manoeuvre to go ahead as planned. There was later testimony that his eyes were strangely dull when he re-issued the order.

At a combined speed of 18 knots, the two lead ships were heading toward each other on a collision course – yet Sir George gave no signal for the turn. He stood like a statue on the charthouse deck, his eyes still vague. When other officers pleaded that they must do something, the admiral failed to answer.

At the last moment, he shook himself like a waking dreamer and whispered, "Yes, go astern." The order was given too late.

Even with the propellers in reverse, the *Victoria*'s momentum carried her like a juggernaut toward the *Camperdown*.

As buglers sounded the call summoning "All hands on deck," the ironclads met in a terrifying collision. *Camperdown* pierced the flagship some 65 feet aft of the bow, on the starboard side. A dreadful shudder racked the *Victoria*.

The ship's pumps might have coped with the torrents of water, but compounding his first ghastly mistake with another, the admiral shouted at *Camperdown*, "Go astern with both engines!"

As the great ship backed away, the fate of the *Victoria* was inevitable. The flagship was swamped by a wall of water that flooded everything in its way; men, machinery and bulkheads.

The ship's hydraulic system was submerged, and below decks hundreds of men were caught in the smothering assault of the seawater. When the order came to report topside, many were either dead or dying in flooded compartments.

Among the 600 who leaped from the ship many were ground to fragments in the propeller blades or trapped in the suction of the foundering *Victoria*. A total of only 25 officers and 259 men were picked up by the boats, with 22 officers and 336 seamen dead.

Among the dead was Sir George Tryon himself, who was still standing on the *Victoria*'s bridge when she slipped beneath the waves.

Spirit of the deep

Trailed by a ghostly galleon

If there are ghosts of people who die, can ships also become spirits too? Captain Dusty Miller came close to answering that question, but he took his knowledge to a watery grave when his yacht, the *Joyita*, sank in 1955. For in the months before his last voyage in the South Seas, something unknown had stalked him and his ship.

Passengers reported that another ship was following in their wake, moving along mysteriously through the darkness with no lights or sound. The ghostly ship had a high superstructure aft, they said, but otherwise could describe her only as looking like an ancient galleon, "from the time of Columbus."

When Captain Miller glimpsed her in his binoculars on a voyage to Pago Pago, his face turned deathly white.

He ordered the running lights turned off and took over the helm himself, heading the *Joyita* into a squall. When the weather cleared there was no sign of the ghostly galleon.

The *Joyita* had the reputation of being an unlucky yacht, and Dusty knew

Cross of mystery

Two boats went to the aid of a strange vessel which was obviously in distress in heavy seas off the coast of Devon in 1959. As they came close to the vessel, they were able to identify it as a World War Two landing craft.

The flag that it was flying was the Cross of Lorraine, the symbol of the Free French forces. As the two boats came still closer, the ship was obscured from view by a sudden giant wave. It never reappeared.

this when he bought her.

Roland West, a film producer with RKO studios, had built her in the first blaze of Hollywood's glory and named her *Joyita* – Spanish for little jewel – in honour of his actress sweetheart Jewel Carmen. The romance fizzled and bad luck began to haunt the yacht even before her launching in 1931.

Workmen fell from the rigging and died. The Portuguese widow of one victim publicly laid a curse on the yacht and its owner.

On her maiden voyage, to Catalina Island, the ship was towed back into port after a disastrous engine room fire.

The *Joyita* was sold and went into charter service. The great stars of the screen were among those who sailed in her. But when a passenger mysteriously vanished, nobody wanted to know the boat any more.

The United States Navy took her over in World War Two, but put her back in dry dock when she kept running aground. Even out of service, her record was grim; a caretaker died from battery acid fumes, there was a series of unexplained fires, and two men were killed in a fight aboard her.

Sold as war surplus, the now shabby yacht went from owner to owner. Dusty Miller bought her with his last few dollars.

On October 3, 1955, the *Joyita* put to sea for the last time from Apia Harbor in Western Samoa. Held in port by order of unhappy creditors, she had almost rusted away for months before Miller could persuade them to let him take her out.

The *Joyita* carried desperately needed food and medical supplies for the islanders of Fakaofo 200 miles north, and she was to bring back 70 tons of copra. Besides the crew of 16, there were nine passengers.

Samoans living on the waterfront later claimed that, minutes after her departure, they saw a huge, dark vessel gliding in the *Joyita*'s wake. She was enormously high aft, and unlike any ship seen in those waters. She was travelling without lights and with no sound of motors, but she moved at an incredible speed.

Nothing was heard of the *Joyita* until November 10, 1955, when another freighter found her lying abandoned 90 miles north of Fiji. She had a 55-degree list to port and one rail was awash.   Radio gear was smashed, the logbook was missing and there was no recognisable message – but carefully-placed signal flags in the rigging spelled out the letters WNQV. To this day investigators have not been able to discover what this may have meant.

No bodies were found in the flooded compartments, and the fate of the 25 persons aboard is still unknown.

In Suva, where the wreck was pumped out, marine inspectors found no answers. The tale of the mysterious ship was put down to native superstition, although it had been government men aboard the *Joyita* who had first reported the ghostly vessel.

But the sailors of the South Sea ports still have no doubts. They still see a clear link between the doomed *Joyita* and the strange, dark galleon from another age.

The Phantom 'Dutchman'
How a King saw a cursed ship

"**A**t 4 am *The Flying Dutchman* crossed our bows. She emitted a strange phosphorescent light as of a phantom ship all aglow, in the midst of which light the masts, spars and sails of a brig 200 yards distant stood out in strong relief as she came up on the port bow, where the officer watch from the bridge saw her, as did the quarter-deck midshipman, who was sent forward at once to the forecastle, but on arriving there no vestige nor any sign whatever of any material ship was to be seen either near or right away to the horizon, the night being clear and the sea calm."

This unsettling apparition was reported in those words by a 16-year-old Royal Navy midshipman aboard the British warship *Inconstant* steaming off the coast of Australia on July 11, 1881. The report might have been put down to the lad's age, inexperience and a youthful imagination – except for one thing. The midshipman was none other than Prince George, later to become King George V of England.

The vision was also seen by 13 other men aboard the *Inconstant* and two sister ships. Later that day the seaman who had first sighted her fell to his death from a mast-top. Some weeks later the Admiral of the Fleet died.

GHOSTS

Over the years, the seagoing belief that bad fortune will dog anyone who sights the *Flying Dutchman* has often been fulfilled. So what – or perhaps who – was the *Flying Dutchman*?

The name originates from the 17th century when an unscrupulously greedy Dutch captain, Hendrik van der Decken, set sail from Amsterdam to seek his fortune in the East Indies. The voyage went smoothly until the Dutch East-Indiaman was rounding the Cape of Good Hope. A fierce storm blew up, ripping the ship's sails to shreds and battering her creaking timbers. But the determined captain pressed on, ignoring the pleas of his crew.

What became of him and his ship is not known, but legend has it that the Devil appeared to the captain and urged him to challenge God's will and sail straight into the storm. The Dutchman agreed and brought upon himself the curse of the Almighty – that he and his ship of living dead should roam the seas without ever making landfall until the Day of Judgement.

Most sightings of the *Flying Dutchman* have been made in the area where legend says she vanished, around the Cape of Good Hope. The phantom vessel has even been spotted from shore.

In March 1939, some 100 people saw the phantom East-Indiaman. They were all sunbathing on Glencairn Beach in False Bay, south-east of Capetown, when a fully rigged sailing ship appeared out of the heat haze. It passed across the bay with its sails full, although there was not a breath of wind. The ship seemed to be heading for a distant, isolated beach. But, as the crowd of excited witnesses looked on, the mysterious *Flying Dutchman* vanished as suddenly as it had appeared.

In September 1942, four people were relaxing on the terrace of their home at Mouille Point, Capetown, when they spotted an ancient sailing ship heading into Table Bay. They followed its progress for about 15 minutes before it disappeared from view behind Robben Island.

The story of the *Flying Dutchman* is fanciful enough. It inspired Wagner's famous opera. But when witnesses of the ghost ship include a future King of England, the sea's best-loved legend becomes difficult to dismiss as just another sailors' yarn.

The ghostly jailer

A phantom policeman patrols Vine Street Police Station in London's City of Westminster. Station Sergeant Goddard hanged himself in one of the cells in the early years of this century, but officers have frequently seen him pounding corridors, opening locked cell doors, and rifling through documents.

Fishermen's fear

For hundreds of years fishermen on the east and south-east coasts of England have kept a watchful eye for a phantom schooner, the *Lady Lovibond*. They wonder how many sailors who met their deaths on the notorious Goodwin Sands had first spied the ghost of the three-master.

The *Lady Lovibond* ran aground on the Goodwins and sank with all hands on February 13, 1748. Captain Simon Peel, his bride and some of their wedding guests were on board. Legend has it that the first mate, who was in love with the bride himself, killed Peel out of jealousy and steered the ship to its doom on the Goodwins.

Fifty years later to the day, a three-masted schooner identical to the *Lady Lovibond* was seen heading for the Goodwins. The crew of a fishing boat followed her and heard the sounds of a celebration and women's voices. The schooner hit the sands, broke up – and vanished.

The same apparition appeared to another ship's crew exactly 50 years later and was next seen by a group of watchers near Deal, Kent, on February 13, 1898.

Does the phantom appear every 50 years? Watchers were on the lookout on February 13, 1948, but visibility was poor and they saw nothing.

North America also has a famous phantom ship lurking off Rhode Island. The *Palatine* left Holland in 1752, packed with colonists bound for Philadelphia. A fierce winter storm blew her off course and, when the captain was lost overboard, the panicking crew mutinied.

The passengers spent Christmas Day in confusion and terror. Two days later, the *Palatine* ran aground on rocks off Block Island and began to break up. As the storm abated, the doomed ship began to slip back off the rocks, drawn out to sea again by the tide. But before she could do so, dozens of local fishermen descended on the *Palatine*, took off the passengers and looted the ship.

When their frenzied rampage had ended and they had stripped the *Palatine* of everything of value, the fishermen set it on fire and watched it drift, ablaze from bow to stern, out to the open sea.

They watched in horror when they saw a woman appear from her hiding place on the *Palatine* and stand on the deck screaming for help until the flames swallowed her.

There have been sightings of the ghostly vessel off the New England coast ever since, blood-red flames rising from a wrecked hulk.

The ghostly swimmers

Seamen James Courtney and Michael Meehan were buried at sea on the morning of December 2, 1929. They had died the previous day, asphyxiated by fumes while working below decks aboard the oil tanker *Waterton*, owned by the Cities Service Corporation, and bound from California to Panama.

When the weighted bodies of the two sailors dropped into the Pacific, their fellow crewmen mourned deeply, for Courtney and Meehan were two of the most popular men on the ship.

One friend said, "Somehow they made everyone feel good."

But the crew of the *Waterton* were not without their dead colleagues for long. The day after their burial, the officers and crew saw two men swimming in the open sea. Captain Tracy put his binoculars on them and whispered, "Oh, my God!"

But when the ship slowed to ten knots and drew up alongside the swimmers, they faded like morning mist – only to reappear just 40 feet from the ship. At that distance there were no longer any doubts. The men in the water were Courtney and Meehan.

For three days the swimmers kept pace with the *Waterton*. Now there was no terror aboard the ship, because everyone saw that the dead men intended no harm. At one point they swam ahead of the vessel and seemed to be trying to divert her from the path of an approaching squall.

Reporting later in the New Orleans office of the shipowners, Captain Tracy told his employers about the death and reappearance of Courtney and Meehan. Tracy was provided with a camera and film and asked to substantiate his tale on the return voyage.

It was a voyage without incident until they were in the Pacific again and the deckhands saw two pale figures bobbing in the wake of the *Waterton*. By dawn they were once more alongside the vessel, and with full light the captain snapped eight pictures at close range. Within a few hours the swimmers had vanished.

They were not seen again in the days that followed, and back in port the captain took the film to company headquarters. Still wet from processing in a photographic laboratory, the roll of film was closely examined in company offices. One by one the negatives were rejected.

Then one of the executives lifted the eighth frame to the light. "There they are!" he said.

When prints were made from the negative, the two pale faces emerging from the waves were positively identified by friends and relatives as those of James Courtney and Michael Meehan.

Terror aboard UB65
Doomed duty of a dead officer

Night was falling at the end of a bitterly cold day in January, 1918, as the German submarine UB65 slid into the English Channel looking for action. She was 15 miles off Portland Bill as the grey winter twilight deepened. The sea was rough and sheets of spray drenched the conning tower.

The U-boat's starboard lookout, screwing up his eyes as he peered over the bridge, was astonished to see an officer standing just below him on the heaving deck.

What in God's name was he doing there? He must be mad. Come to that, how on earth did he get there anyway? All the hatches save that on the conning tower had been firmly battened down.

He was about to hail the officer to warn him that he was in great danger when the figure on the deck turned and gazed up at the bridge. Even in the twilight, the lookout recognised the face, and his blood froze.

It was the ship's former second officer, killed in an explosion on the maiden voyage, his body buried in the military cemetery at Wilhelmshaven.

It seemed hours before he could move his lips. "It's the ghost," he yelled. The U-boat's captain rushed to his side, and he too saw the upturned face, before the figure melted into the gathering darkness.

This was not the first time that the phantom of UB65 had appeared to strike terror into the hearts of the men who sailed in her. They had begun to dread the ghost as a harbinger of doom.

Ever since her keel was laid, disaster had followed disaster until UB65 became known as a jinxed ship. The submarine had been built in 1916, one of a fleet designed to operate off the coast of Flanders and create havoc in the Channel. Her crew was made up of three officers and 31 ratings.

Only a week after work started on her, things began to go wrong. A girder being swung into position slipped from its chains and crashed down killing one workman outright and pinning another to the ground. He could not be released for an hour and then died in agony.

Before the submarine was finished there was another accident, this time in the engine room. Three men, overcome by fumes, died before they could be rescued.

On her trial run UB65 ran into a fierce storm and a man was washed overboard. While she was on diving tests, one of the tanks developed a leak and it was 12 hours before she could be brought to the surface. The atmosphere was thick with poisonous fumes and when at last the hatches were opened officers and men staggered out half dead with suffocation.

But it was on her return from her maiden voyage that the UB65 suffered her most violent shock. As she was taking in torpedoes a warhead exploded and in the terrible explosion that followed the second officer was killed and several men badly injured. The officer was buried with full naval honours and the submarine had to go into the dockyard for repairs.

Some weeks later, just before the vessel was due to sail, a member of the crew crashed unceremoniously into the wardroom. Chalk white with shock, he gasped out, "Herr Ober-Leutnant, the dead officer is on board." The captain accused him of being drunk, but he swore that not only he but another rating had seen the dead officer walk up the gangplank.

The captain and other officers ran to the deck where they found the second seaman crouching against the conning tower. He explained in a voice barely above a whisper that the dead officer had come on board, walked towards the bows and stood there with folded arms. After a few seconds, he vanished.

The captain, fully aware of the impact such an incident would have on his superstitious crew, circulated the rumour that the whole thing had been a practical joke. Nobody believed him. Everyone knew the ship was haunted.

On each tour of duty the U-boat carried its ghostly second officer. Men on watch jumped at every shadow. Word spread throughout the German navy that the UB65 was haunted and nobody was anxious to serve on her.

Eventually, the authorities felt it was time such nonsense was stopped and sent a commodore to investigate. The high-ranking officer questioned the entire company. At first he could hardly conceal his impatience with what he believed was superstitious fancy. After hearing all the evidence, he was so impressed that he admitted he could understand the request by almost every member of the crew to transfer to another ship. Officially, the requests were never granted, but one by one men were switched.

The UB65 was withdrawn from active service and, while in dock at the Belgian port of Bruges, a Lutheran pastor was quietly taken aboard to carry out the rite of exorcism. When she went to sea again the U-boat had a new captain and crew. This captain refused to tolerate what he called "damn nonsense" and threatened any man who spoke of ghosts with severe penalties. Strangely enough, the ship carried out two tours of duty without trouble, but when the unbeliever was replaced, the spirit reappeared. The next trip was worst of all.

During May of 1918, the UB65 cruised in the Channel and later off the coast of Spain. The ghost was seen three times. A young petty officer swore he saw an unfamiliar officer walk into the torpedo room. He never came out again. After two more sightings, the torpedo gunner went mad, screaming that the ghost would not leave him alone. He threw himself over the side and his body was never recovered.

In spite of her terrible history, the UB65 managed to escape the massive onslaught on the U-boats which came in the final months of war. On July 10, an American submarine patrolling at periscope depth spotted her on the surface. The Americans prepared to attack and were on the point of firing when the UB65 blew up. The explosion was "tremendous, almost unbelievable," said eye witnesses. When the smoke cleared all that was left was debris.

Many rational theories were put forward to explain what had happened. It was suggested that the submarine had been rammed by another German sub or perhaps the UB65 herself had fired a torpedo that ran wild. But spectators admitted that none of them quite accounted for the force of the explosion.

The nearest anyone could guess was that by some means the mouth of a torpedo tube had been damaged so that when one was fired it fouled and detonated the rest of the torpedoes in the craft.

The company of 34 men went down with the UB65 – or maybe it was 35, for the ghost of the second officer was never seen again.

Perhaps he had finished the terrible job he had stayed on earth to do.

The ghost ship Ourang Medan

Adozen ships picked up the SOS, which read, "Captain and all officers dead. Entire crew dead or dying." And later, "Now I am also near death." Then the airwaves went dead.

It was a perfect day in February 1948 and, of all the vessels that heard the strange message, only one was able to identify the ship in trouble and pinpoint her position. The ship was named as the Dutch freighter *Ourang Medan*, bound for Djakarta, Indonesia, through the Malacca Strait.

Within three hours, the first rescue vessel was alongside the *Ourang Medan*. A crewman said later, "Sharks were surging around the hull, and it looked like every shark in the Bay of Bengal had homed in on her knowing there was death aboard."

When there was no response to flag or radio signals, a boat was launched and the rescue party climbed aboard. They found all the ship's officers massed in the chartroom as if their skipper had called them to a council of war against some unknown disaster. All had died there.

They seemed to have died within seconds of each other; their eyes stared in horror and their bodies were already locked in rigor mortis, some with their arms pointed to the heavens.

The dead seamen littering the decks had died in the same way. A doctor who boarded with the party later reported no signs of poisoning, asphyxiation or disease, but all seemed to have known that death was coming – even the ship's dog. They found it below decks with paws in the air, fangs bared in a silent snarl. In the radio shack, the telegrapher had fallen over his silent key.

The rescue ship tried to take the Dutch ship in tow to the nearest port, but when tackle had been readied and a towline rigged, there was a gush of oily smoke from one of the holds. Knowing they could not contain the blaze without flushing pumps and steam for the fire, the salvage crew fled to their own ship. They had only time enough to cut the towline before the stricken freighter exploded.

The blast scattered wreckage for a quarter of a mile and even killed some of the hungry sharks. What was left of the *Ourang Medan* sank.

In the short inquiry that followed, the doctor reported that something unknown had killed the seamen. Although the official verdict was "death by misadventure", the mystery of the ghost ship *Ourang Medan* has never been solved.

The mystery of the Mary Celeste

The most famous ghost ship of all time is the *Mary Celeste*. More than a century after her bizarre discovery, drifting and devoid of life in the middle of the Atlantic, no one is any nearer solving the mystery.

Mary Celeste, a square-rigged brigantine, pointed her bows out of New York's East River on November 4, 1872, bound for Genoa, in Italy, with a cargo of crude alcohol. Aboard were her 37-year-old American master, Benjamin Spooner Briggs, her first mate, Albert Richardson, and a crew of seven. Also tucked safely below decks were the captain's wife, Sarah, and their two-year-old daughter Sophia.

On November 24, Briggs recorded in his log that he had sighted the Azores. The weather was stormy and some of the sails were furled. The following morning the ship's bearings were noted in the log.

It was the last entry ever made.

Ten days later the British brigantine, the *Dei Gratia*, sighted the *Mary Celeste* drifting aimlessly. Captain David Morehouse ordered a longboat to be launched to investigate. The three crewmen who rowed across to the mysterious ship found not a single man, woman or child aboard – living or dead.

In the captain's cabin was Mrs Briggs' rosewood melodeon with a sheet of music still on it as if someone had left in a hurry halfway through a piece. The sewing machine was on a table. Little Sophia's toys were neatly stowed. In the crew's quarters washing hung on a line. Clothing lay on bunks, dry and undisturbed. In the galley, preparations seemed to have been made for breakfast, although only half of it appeared to have been served.

Captain Morehouse, mindful of the salvage value of the vessel, took the *Mary Celeste* in tow. As they headed for Gibraltar, he had time to ponder on his mysterious discovery. As he put forward theories for the riddle of the *Mary Celeste*, so he found arguments for dismissing them.

Morehouse first thought that the ship must have been abandoned in a storm. But why then was there an open and unspilled bottle of cough medicine along with the unbroken plates and ornaments in the captain's cabin?

A mutiny, perhaps? There was no sign of a struggle – and why should the mutineers abandon ship along with their victims?

Perhaps the ship had been taking water? There was three feet of water in the hold, but this would be the normal intake over ten days for any old timber-hulled ship.

Nine of the casks of alcohol were found to be dry, but a further cask had been breached. Could the crew have gone on a drunken rampage? Yet below decks the ship had been in perfect order. In fact, there was no sign of panic or alarm. One of the last acts of Captain Briggs had been to cut the top neatly off his boiled egg before leaving it uneaten on his plate.

The most baffling question of all was this: How was the *Mary Celeste* able to remain on course without a crew for ten days and 500 miles? When the *Dei Gratia* caught up with the mystery ship, Captain Morehouse was sailing on a port tack. The *Mary Celeste* was on a starboard tack. It was inconceivable that the mystery ship could have travelled the course she did with her sails set that way. Someone must have been aboard her for several days after her last log entry.

Captain Morehouse towed the *Mary Celeste* into Gibraltar harbour on December 13. After an inconclusive public inquiry, he and his men were awarded the salvage money they had sought.

The ship was refitted and sold. But she remained ill-fated. Sailors refused to sail in her, believing the vessel to be cursed. She changed hands 17 times before finally running aground and sinking on a coral reef off Haiti in 1884.

The Devil's Triangle

Tormented souls may hold Bermuda key

A startling theory to explain the mysterious disappearance of ships and planes in the notorious Bermuda Triangle is that the strange happenings in that region are caused by tormented souls from the spirit world.

The claim is made by two leading exorcists who believe that the "spirits" in the area known as the Triangle of Death, the Devil's Triangle and the Hoodoo Sea are from ten million negroes who were dumped or thrown overboard during the slave trade period. Their troubled souls can "take over" the minds of pilots and sailors, just as people on land are said to be possessed by spirits.

In a unique experiment, special prayers were held in the Bermuda Triangle to lay at peace these tormented souls who supposedly haunt the

Atlantic graveyard of 140 ships and planes and more than 1,000 people who over the years have disappeared without trace.

Backing this extraordinary theory is British surgeon and psychiatrist Dr Kenneth McCall. He said, "We call it the Possession Syndrome in patients who are mentally disturbed.

"It may be multiple or single, in a family or haunted place. The spirits have got to express themselves, so they possess us and control our minds.

"Just as in our world here, one or two people can cause torment or haunting disturbances. This can happen with the crew of a ship or plane – and on a very large scale in the Bermuda Triangle. It seems the spirits are trying to draw attention to their state. They are not concerned with destroying the other people.

"There is no such thing as time and space to the spirits. They are wandering and lost and possess people to draw attention to their own plight, just as a lost child will do to an adult.

"These unhappy lost spirits are in purgatory. Because they did not die naturally and were not committed to God, they are causing disturbance."

Dr McCall, at the age of 67, wrote a special service to be said over the troubled waters and this included the Requiem Mass and the Anglican Eucharist of Remembrance.

He said, "I think this will lessen the number of planes and ships that disappear there."

Dr McCall carried out 600 cases of exorcism, or laying on of hands, in the United States, Canada, Holland, Germany and Switzerland. He was a member of a Church of England Commission on Exorcism in Britain. He made many visits to America and with 12 American professors wrote a book on the subject.

It was after working as a missionary in China, where he was imprisoned, that he found he could cure other prisoners through the power of prayer.

He said, "When I returned to Britain in 1946 and learnt all about psychiatry, I realised that the same results occurred in mental hospitals. The patients were disturbed because they were possessed by a spirit."

His theory that millions of disturbed spirits are in the Bermuda Triangle – the area bounded roughly by Bermuda in the north to Miami and beyond Puerto Rico – came to him when he was becalmed on a small banana boat in the Sargasso Sea.

He said, "I had been on a lecture tour in the States and visiting relatives. The ship's boiler burst and we were drifting. It was calm and peaceful and I heard singing. I thought it was the coloured crew, but I couldn't think why they were singing all the time."

Dr McCall checked and found that none of the crew was singing and there was not even a record player aboard. "Then I realised it was a negro dirge, like a moaning chant. It went on and on solidly for five days and nights before we got moving again. My wife Frances also heard it. What we heard fitted all my other theories."

He believes that during the slave trade years, about ten million slaves went overboard. "They used to push them over because they got more money from insurance that way. Those who were pregnant or diseased were thrown to the sharks. Others preferred to jump over the side rather than die in slavery."

Of the many mysteries of the Bermuda Triangle, the most famous is that of the missing warplanes. It is also the case that first aroused widespread public curiosity and gave the area its name.

On December 5, 1945, a flight of five Grumann United States Navy bombers took off from Fort Lauderdale, Florida, for a training flight in perfect weather. Shortly afterwards, the pilots radioed that they were on course, although they were actually flying in the opposite direction. Two hours after take-off, all contact with the aircraft was lost.

A Martin bomber was immediately sent to search for the missing planes. Within 20 minutes, radio contact with it had also been lost. No trace of any of the aircraft was ever found. In all, six planes and 27 men simply vanished into thin air.

In Dr McCall's view, the leader of the training flight believed to the last that he was heading in the right direction, but that his judgement was distorted by spirits.

The spirit theory had been current among seamen for many years before the world heard of the Triangle. The greatest disaster in the area had taken place 27 years earlier, in March 1918. That was the month in which the US supply vessel *Cyclops* vanished from the face of the earth without making a single distress call. No wreckage or any of the crew of 309 was ever found.

The service and prayers aimed at ending such disasters were carried out in

---

The ghost of Grace Darling

Two lighthouse-keepers told television viewers in 1976 that they had both seen the ghost of Grace Darling on separate occasions. The men worked at the Longstone Lighthouse on the Farne Islands, off the Northumberland Coast.

Grace was born there in 1815 and became a national hero 23 years later when she and her father rowed out to rescue nine survivors from the storm-wrecked steamer Forfarshire. Grace died of consumption four years later. The men said they had seen her ghost in the lighthouse engine room, walking round in clogs.

the Bermuda Triangle by exorcist Donald Omand, a 74-year-old retired Church of England vicar and expert on the occult, who described himself as a spiritual surgeon. In previous exorcisms, he had driven spirits from people, buildings and animals.

Dr McCall was unable to go with him to the Triangle, but Omand was accompanied by an English doctor and writer Marc Alexander, who said, "The Rev Omand often works with medical men and psychiatrists. Nearly all his cases are referred to him by doctors.

"This is a sensational subject and my eyes were opened by a lot of the things he did."

Omand's work of laying spirits at rest has been supported by Peter Mumford, the Bishop of Hertford, who said, "He was a member of a church commission which reported a few years ago on exorcism. He is a recognised exorcist and an expert in this field. He is very experienced and well regarded and has contributed to our understanding of this field."

But whether he has placated the "spirits" of the Bermuda Triangle, only time will reveal.

'Help me in the name of God'

A woman's ghostly cries for help are the only clues to the disappearance of a Mississippi riverboat that vanished 106 years ago. The strange voice was first reported on the evening of May 28, 1875. Picnicking near the riverbank, more than 50 Vicksburgh high school students told police they had heard a woman screaming for help somewhere on the river.

The police decided it was a prank. They made a thorough search of the waters, but there was no such woman. There has been no such woman in 106 years, though hundreds of different people have reported the same eerie cries. The reports have come from Vicksburgh, Natchez, St Joseph and other points along the Mississippi.

In most documented cases, the chilling screams are followed by words in French, "*Aidez-moi au nom de Dieu, les hommes me blessent!*" ("Help me in the name of God, the men are hurting me!")

No one can explain the disembodied voice or its message, but there are fishermen and residents of the riverbank communities who believe it is linked to a darker mystery that still haunts the "father of waters".

On a clear blue day in June, 1874, the riverboat, *Iron Mountain* set out from Vicksburgh for New Orleans carrying 57 passengers and towing a string of barges. The big paddle-wheel steamer was famous in her time, plying the Ohio and Mississippi rivers to every port between New Orleans and Pittsburgh.

But on this voyage, she was sailing into history, for after rounding a bend in the river, she vanished.

Not long after her departure, the string of barges was found bobbing in the water. The towropes had been slashed in two – something that would be done only in an emergency. But no emergency had been reported, and rescue craft converging on the scene could find no evidence of one.

Hundreds of miles of river bottom were dragged, but the waters yielded no trace of wreckage or bodies.

Of the many explanations advanced at the time, one has often reappeared through the years. In that troubled period after the Civil War, riverboat pirates still operated on some parts of the Mississippi, and there was tempting cargo of wealth and beauty aboard the *Iron Mountain*.

On the passenger list were several Creole women who spoke French. Could the big steamboat have been sacked by pirates who dismantled her and concealed the sections after a ghastly carnival of rape and murder?

Voyage of the frozen dead

The Yankee whaling ship *Herald* was cruising off the west coast of Greenland, inside the Arctic Circle. From the bridge, Captain Warren peered ahead at a three-masted schooner drifting through the ice floes like a ghost ship. Warren took eight men in a longboat and rowed to the silent vessel. Through the encrusted ice, they could make out the schooner's name: *Octavius*.

Warren and four of the sailors boarded the schooner. They crossed the silent, moss-covered decks, opened a hatch and descended to the crew's quarters. There they found the bodies of 28 men, all lying on their bunks and wrapped in heavy blankets.

They fumbled their way aft to the captain's cabin, where the nightmare continued. The master of the *Octavius* slumped over the ship's log, a pen close to his right hand as if he had dozed at work. On a bed against one wall of the cabin, a blonde woman lay frozen to death under piles of blankets. And in a corner there were a sailor and a small boy whose bodies told a tragic story.

The sailor sat with his flint and steel clutched in frozen hands. In front of him was a tiny heap of shavings, silent evidence of a fire that had failed to ignite. The little boy crouched close to him, his face buried in the seaman's jacket as if he had huddled there in pathetic search for warmth.

The men from the *Herald* clambered back onto the deck, taking with them the schooner's log book as proof of what they had found. Back aboard the whaler, they could only watch helplessly while the derelict schooner drifted away from them among the icebergs, never to be seen again.

It was well they had taken the log book. The world would not be ready to accept their story, which remains one of the strangest tales of the sea.

The last log entry was dated November 11, 1762. The dying captain wrote that the *Octavius* had been frozen in for 17 days. The fire had gone out and they could not restart it. The location of the ship at this time, said the captain, was Longitude 160W, Latitude 75N.

Captain Warren looked at the charts in disbelief. In those last hours of human life, the ship had been locked in the Arctic Ocean north of Point Barrow, Alaska – thousands of miles from where the whaler had found her. Guided by some unknown force, year after year the battered schooner had crept steadily eastward through the vast ice fields until she entered the North Atlantic. In doing so she had then achieved the dream of all mariners.

For centuries men had sought the legendary Northwest Passage – a navigable route around the Arctic Ocean between the Atlantic and the Pacific. On that historic 13-year voyage, the ghost ship *Octavius* with her crew of frozen dead had been the first to find it.

Screams of a betrayer

Britain's coastline is rich in salty tales of smuggling exploits, and many towns with rocky caves nearby claim they are haunted by the ghosts of contraband runners.

One such story is told of Marsden Grotto, a series of caverns between South Shields and Sunderland, on England's north-eastern coast.

The gang using the Grotto to land their booty were betrayed by one of their colleagues, a man called John the Jibber. Coastguards were waiting when they rowed their loot ashore from a lugger anchored in Marsden Bay. A friend of the smugglers got wind of the plot, and fired a pistol, alerting those aboard the lugger that something had gone wrong.

John the Jibber lived to regret his treachery. He was trussed up in a barrel, hoisted to the roof of the cavern, and left to starve to death. The Grotto – now a restaurant – has echoed with his screams for more than 150 years.

The lonely lighthouse

On the night the Eilean Mor Lighthouse went dark, two sailors on the brigantine *Fairwind* saw a strange sight. Cutting diagonally across their bow a longboat with a huddle of men aboard was bearing toward the lighthouse on the rocky Flannan Islands off the west coast of Scotland.

The sailors called, but there was no answer. The boatmen wore foul weather gear and when moonlight slashed through a rift in the clouds, their faces shone like bone. One of the would-be rescuers testified later, "Our first thought was that they were floating dead from some shipwreck. But then we heard the oarlocks and saw the movement of their arms."

Later on that night of December 15, 1900, a squall broke. Without the guardian light ships were in dire peril. There was one angry question from the skippers: Why was the lighthouse dark?

On the day after Christmas, the supply vessel *Hesperus* hove to off the islands to investigate. When there was no answer to repeated signals, crewmen set out in a small boat to the landing dock. Tying up, they were chilled by the strange silence.

The lighthouse had been staffed by three men, but no one was there to welcome the *Hesperus*. There were no signs of violence and the larders were well stocked. Lamps were all trimmed and ready, the beds made, the dishes and kitchen utensils shining.

As the searchers climbed through the empty lighthouse, they found only two things that struck them as unusual. On the stairway and in a cubbyhole office where the log was kept, there were shreds of a seaweed unknown to them.

There were no oilskins or seaboots in the building, which seemed to imply that all three men had left the lighthouse together.

No lighthouse keeper had ever been known to abandon his post, even in the worst weather, and this was a point repeatedly made during the inquiry which followed – an inquiry which was hushed to silence by the reading of the log book kept by keeper Thomas Marshall:

"December 12: Gale north by northwest. Sea lashed to fury. Never seen such a storm. Waves very high. Tearing at lighthouse. Everything shipshape. James Ducat irritable." And later that day: "Storm still raging, wind steady. Stormbound. Cannot go out. Ship passing sounding foghorn. Could see lights of cabins. Ducat quiet. Donald McArthur crying.

"December 13: Storm continued through night. Wind shifted west by north. Ducat quiet. McArthur praying." And later: "Noon, grey daylight. Me, Ducat and McArthur prayed."

Inexplicably, there was no entry for December 14. The final line in the log read: "December 15, 1 pm. Storm ended, sea calm. God is over all."

No explanation could be offered but that the men had been seeing visions. While the log entries had reported gales lashing the Flannan Isles, there had been none at all 20 miles away on the island of Lewis.

Locals pointed to an even more mysterious cause of the disappearance of the lighthouse men. For centuries, the Flannan Isles had been haunted. Hebridean farmers might sail there during daylight to check on their sheep – but few except the "foolish sassenachs" at the lighthouse dared stay overnight.

Final "proof", if the locals needed any, was the evidence of the sailors of the *Fairwind* – of the longboat crowded with ghosts.

Chapter Five

Ghosts of the Highways and Skyways

There are Rolls-Royce Phantom cars and many air forces fly Phantom jets. There are also less tangible phantoms on our roads and in the sky. Twentieth century technology has discovered ways to let us journey where and when we want to. But it cannot explain why we may meet Bronze Age horsemen along the way. Or why dead pilots sometimes appear out of thin air . . .

Legend of the hairy hands

Holidaymaker Florence Warwick had never heard of the ghostly hands that are supposed to terrify victims on Dartmoor in Devon, but she discovered all she would ever want to know when her car broke down on the moor one evening.

Florence, aged 28, was driving along the lonely road from Postbridge to Two Bridges after a sightseeing tour. When the car started to judder she pulled over to the side of the road to look at the handbook.

She recalled: "As I was reading in the failing light, a cold feeling suddenly came over me. I felt as if I was being watched. I looked up and saw a pair of huge, hairy hands pressed against the windscreen. I tried to scream, but couldn't. I was frozen with fear."

She watched wide-eyed as the disembodied hands that are said to have haunted this desolate place for 60 years began to crawl across the windscreen. "It was horrible, they were just inches away," she said. "After what seemed a lifetime, I heard myself cry out and the hands seemed to vanish."

Florence was so shaken she hardly noticed that her car started first time. By the time she had driven the 20 miles back to Torbay, where she was staying with friends, she began to think she had imagined the whole incident. But then her friends told her the legend of the hands.

The "curse" on the road began to be felt in the early 1920s. Pony traps were overturned, a cyclist felt his handlebars wrenched from his grasp and ran full tilt into a stone wall, horses shied and bolted. A doctor travelling on a motor-cycle with two children in the sidecar was nearly killed when the engine literally detached itself from the machine. An Army officer reported an enormous pair of hands covered in long dark hairs taking charge of his steering wheel, covering his own.

Things reached a head in 1921 when a newspaper sent investigators to the spot and the local authority had the camber of the road altered. But the hands refused to be deterred.

Not long after the road improvement a young couple were visiting the area with their caravan. As is common on Dartmoor, a heavy fog suddenly fell one evening as they were driving towards Plymouth. Rather than drive on and risk losing their way, the couple decided to park in a lay-by along the Postbridge road. They cooked themselves a snack and settled down to sleep.

The woman had only been asleep for a short time when she was awakened by a strange scratching noise which seemed to be coming from outside the caravan. Thinking it might be a dog wandering lost on the moors, she got out of bed to take a look. Suddenly a strange chill came over her and she turned to look at the window above her husband's bunk.

There, slowly crawling across glass right above her sleeping husband, was an enormous pair of hairy hands. The woman was too stunned even to cry out, but for some inexplicable reason, as she sat rigid with fear staring at the gruesome apparition, she made the sign of the cross and the hands vanished.

The incident was the talk of the county, and it gave rise to the inevitable jokes and hoaxes. Soon enough the local police began to ignore reports that came in, attributing many of the sightings to an over-indulgence in the local cider. But in 1960 a fatal accident on the lonely stretch of road raised again the spectre of the hands.

A motorist driving from Plymouth to Chagford was found dead beneath the wreckage of his overturned car. No other car was involved and there seemed to be no reason, other than a fault in the car itself, that could have caused the vehicle to career off the road. But when police experts examined the wreckage they could find no mechanical fault in the car. It is a mystery which has never been solved.

Motorists are not the only ones to have suffered the attentions of this unusual manifestation. Walkers making their way along the stretch of road have reported strange experiences and sensations even though they have never heard of the legend of the hands.

One hiker enjoying the rugged beauty of the scenery got carried away during his walk and found himself making his way along the road at dusk. Suddenly he was overcome by an inexplicable feeling of panic, he was rooted to the spot, yet he could see no reason for his sense of fear. Minutes later the feeling passed and he carried on his way puzzling over his strange experience. Only later did he hear the story of the hauntings.

Nobody has been able to explain the strange happenings on this lonely stretch of highway. The only clue to the appearance of the hairy disembodied hands is that in the far distant past a Bronze Age village stood along the once-busy but now-sinister Dartmoor road.

Girl in a raincoat

A limping blonde girl in a pale raincoat has startled several motorists on the A23 road north of Brighton, Sussex. In 1964 one driver saw her dash to the central reservation and vanish. In 1972, several people said they saw her north of the village of Pyecombe. She may be the ghost of a young girl killed in a motor cycle accident in the area.

Ghost fliers of the Florida sky

Aircrew came back from the dead

"You may unfasten your seatbelts." The indicator lights in the bulkheads above the passengers went out. At the rear of Eastern Airlines Tri-Star 318, stewardess Fay Merryweather left her seat near the emergency exit and went to the galley. There was less than two hours to serve the 180 sunseekers heading from New York to the holiday beaches of Florida.

In the galley, Fay reached for the handle of the oven door, and as she did so, she fell back, stunned, against the galley wall as though hit by an electric shock. Staring at her from the glass door of the oven was the face of a man. The image wavered. Then the lips moved, but Fay heard nothing. Her hands were clasped, her mouth fell open, but somehow she stopped herself screaming. It wasn't true, it wasn't true. It couldn't be!

Fay shut her eyes, then opened them. There was nothing there. She had imagined it. She took a deep breath. The in-flight meals must be served. She leaned forward again towards the oven door, then reached for the handle.

There it was again, blurred at first, then forming solid lines. It was the same face. The mouth moved, the eyes blinked. A frown furrowed the brow, a look of urgency crossed the phantom face.

Fay staggered from the galley, her brain swirling. You mustn't panic, she told herself. Was she sure of what she had seen? Do not alarm the passengers. The lessons of her training flooded through her head. She smoothed her skirt, swallowed a lungful of air, and walked as steadily as she could to the flight deck.

Fay shook the flight engineer's shoulder. "Quick," she said, "there's a problem."

She gave him no time to think, but strode back down the aisle towards the galley. The engineer followed, puzzled. At the door of the galley, Fay gripped his arm. She said it as matter-of-factly as she could.

"There's a ghost, a man's face. It's in the oven door."

The engineer stepped in front of the oven, leaned forward, and stared into a face he knew, the face of his Eastern Airlines former colleague, flight engineer Don Repo who had been dead for a year.

Then, beneath the whine of the Tri-Star engines, and just audible in the metallic cell that was the galley, a voice whispered, "Beware, beware. Fire in the jet." The words faded with the face.

Fay made the report in the unemotive words of unsuperstitious crew members who knew the dangers of the job and were too down-to-earth to believe in fantasies.

Neither she nor the flight engineer travelled in Tri-Star 318 again. Months later, the plane developed engine trouble on a flight to Mexico. It returned to New York for repairs and trials. As it took off for a routine test flight, an engine burst into flames.

At Washington's Flight Safety Foundation, records of the Federal Aviation Agency's report on the incident shows that only luck and the skill of the flight maintenance crew got the plane down without loss of life. Packed with passengers, it could have been a disaster.

The startled aircrew of Tri-Star 318 were not the only Eastern Airlines Tri-Star staff to come face to face with one of the Ghost Fliers of the Florida Skies – spirits who haunted the airline's great planes to prevent horrors like the one that hurled them into limbo.

The story began on a warm autumn day in 1972 as the sun glittered on the patchy swamps of the Florida Everglades, and a soft, southern breeze gently bent the swamp grass.

In the sky above, Captain Bob Loft and Flight Engineer Don Repo were bringing their Lockheed L-1011 Tri-Star, Flight 401 from New York to Miami, to the end of a routine journey. The 176 passengers were ready to fasten their seatbelts.

The order to activate the undercarriage was carried out. Bob Loft studied the panel of instruments. Strange, the indicator light showed that nothing had happened. The nosewheel should have lowered and locked. But the small light which should have confirmed this had not come on.

Bob Loft put the aircraft on to a circling course and locked in the automatic pilot while Don Repo scrambled into an observation bay, from where he could see if the wheel was locked into position. Meanwhile, Loft decided to check the indicator light bulb for a fault. He swivelled around in his seat to reach the light cover. He took his eyes off the panels and the flight path in front of him as he tried to unscrew the bulb. As Loft twisted he had without knowing it, knocked off the automatic pilot switch.

He was still fixing the light bulb, when something made him look up. Through the cockpit windscreen there was the flash of glinting water speeding past. One glance told him the frightening message from the instrument panel, but there was no time to do or say anything. Flight 401 smashed into the swamps in a stream of flying water, mud and vegetation. Bob Loft, Don Repo and 97 other people died.

The plane was not entirely smashed. Some parts were hardly damaged. Seats, and the galley in the rear of the plane were in sufficiently good

---

The phantom airfield

Flying over Southern England in 1937, a young RAF pilot, later to become Air Marshal Sir Victor Goddard, looked out of the cockpit of his plane and spotted an airfield with hangars and aircraft. He was puzzled for the place was not recorded on maps and charts and he reported his sighting.

Five years later Goddard saw the place again – shortly after it was built, exactly where he had seen it, as part of the RAF's front-line against the Nazis.

---

condition to be salvaged. Accident inspectors sent them back to Lockheed, where they were reconstructed. Down on the factory assembly line, the parts were built into new Tri-Stars.

The galley was fitted into No 318.

Early in 1973, 318 was airborne and an Eastern Airlines vice-president flew in it, along with airline staff being ferried back as passengers from destinations where their duties had ended. Cabin staff had checked in an off-duty captain, who was sitting in the first class compartment. The vice-president joined him. They chatted amiably for a while.

The captain suddenly turned and looked full face at the airline chief, who gasped. It was Bob Loft.

The vice-president dashed from his seat to seek help from the cabin staff. But when a stewardess returned with him, the seat was empty. The ghost fliers were riding the skies.

The next mysterious visitation occurred when a startled flight engineer stepped onto the flight deck to check the instruments before a routine Florida trip.

A uniformed officer was already in his seat, and he turned to face the duty engineer. The face was unmistakably that of Don Repo. His voice said, "You don't have to check the instruments. I've already done that."

Weeks later an Eastern Airlines captain, aware of the flight engineer's report on the eerie cockpit incident, decided to check the instruments himself before taking off from Miami for Atlanta, Georgia. He ran through the checks, but staring at him from the face of the panel was the ghostly, wavering outline of Don Repo's face.

Then came words like a distant echo. "There will never be another crash on an L-1011. We will not let it happen."

One other captain saw the ghostly travellers of Eastern Airlines, and a stewardess, sent to check smoke coming from a Tri-Star bulkhead during a flight, came face to face with the misty figure of dead pilot Bob Loft.

The Flight Safety Foundation has studied detailed reports of the ghost sightings. Liaison executive Doris Ahnstrom said, "The reports were given by experienced and trustworthy pilots and aircrew. We consider them significant.

"The appearance of the dead flight engineer in the Tri-Star galley door was confirmed by the flight engineer. Later records at the Federal Aviation Agency record the fire which broke out on that same Tri-Star. We published reports of the ghost sightings in our safety bulletin issued to airlines in 1974."

The ghost appearances of the dead fliers ended after 18 months, following an amazing ceremony in the galley of the haunted jet, Tri-Star 318. A religious devotee, who was also a technical second officer with Eastern Airlines, was granted permission to hold an exorcism ceremony.

Aircrew, distressed by the increasing frequency of the apparitions, recited prayers. The officer sprinkled water in the galley and, as he did so, the anguished face of Don Repo stared despairingly at him.

The ghost fliers of the Florida skies were never seen again.

Cursed car of Sarajevo

Archduke Franz Ferdinand wanted a car that would impress the public when he and his wife, the lovely Duchess of Hohenburgh, toured the tiny Bosnian capital of Sarajevo. There were reasons for putting on a brave show. Europe seethed with political unrest, and the Archduke's goodwill trip could be hazardous.

The royal couple arrived at Sarajevo on June 28, 1914, in a blood-red, six-seat open tourer. It made a splendid target. A young fanatic armed with a pistol leaped onto the running board of the car. Laughing in the faces of the Archduke and Duchess, he fired shot after shot into their bodies.

The double assassination was the spark that touched off the Great War, with its casualty list of 20 million.

After the Armistice, the newly appointed Governor of Yugoslavia had the car restored to first-class condition, but after four accidents and the loss of his right arm, he felt the vehicle should be destroyed.

His friend Dr Srikis disagreed. Scoffing at the notion that a car could be cursed, he drove it happily for six months – till the overturned vehicle was found on the highway with the doctor's crushed body beneath it.

Another doctor became the next owner, but when his superstitious patients began to desert him, he hastily sold it to a Swiss racing driver. In a road race in the Dolomites, the car threw him over a stone wall and he died of a broken neck.

A well-to-do farmer then acquired the car, which stalled one day. While another farmer was towing it in for repairs, the vehicle suddenly growled into full power and knocked the tow-car aside, killing both farmers.

Tiber Hirshfield, the car's last private owner, decided that all the old vehicle needed was a less sinister colour scheme. He had it repainted in a cheerful blue and invited five friends to accompany him to a wedding. Hirshfield and four of his guests died in a head-on smash as they drove to the festivities.

The Archduke Franz Ferdinand and his wife 20 minutes before they were assassinated.

Finally the rebuilt car was shipped to a Vienna museum where it was lovingly cared for by attendant Karl Brunner, who revelled in the stories about the car's "curse" and forbade any visitor to sit in it.

During World War Two, bombs reduced the museum to rubble. Nothing was found of the car – or of Karl Brunner.

Check-in for terror

G hosts are normally associated with lonely moors, eerie castles or old mansions, but London's Heathrow Airport is haunted by not one ghost but three.

Airline girls have been terrified by an invisible ghost that pants like a dog. They say it creeps up behind them and breathes down their necks – at a spot said to have been haunted by the spirit of highwayman Dick Turpin.

One Pan American employee said, "I had just left my car in the staff park when the panting started. It sounded like an animal. I turned round but there was nothing there. The panting got close – right up to my neck. When I turned round again two other people, a girl and a man, had moved away. They had exactly the same experience."

An airline engineer said, "A lot of people have heard the weird noises and there seems no logical explanation."

The second ghost that haunts the airport is not invisible. It doesn't pant, but is just as frightening. It is known as "the ghost in the light grey suit."

One man who saw the ghost was a distinguished diplomat from an African high commission in London. He fled from one of the airport's VIP lounges.

The ghost appears in the VIP suite at the airport's European Terminal 1, which is used by the Queen, foreign heads of state and ambassadors.

A catering supervisor said, "The African diplomat was petrified. All we could get out of him was that he had seen the bottom half of a man in grey trousers standing in front of him. Ever since, he has refused to go anywhere near the area."

The supervisor believes she saw the ghost in grey on another occasion. "When I looked again he had vanished," she said. "There was no way he could have got out of the lounge without coming past me. I'm not afraid. I think he's friendly."

An airport policewoman is another who has experienced a strange "presence" in the lounge. She said, "I'm a sceptic about the supernatural, but I can't explain this."

A bowler-hatted ghost has been seen on Runway 1 at Heathrow many times over the last 20 years. A spiritualist once described the figure as that of a Guardsman, about six feet tall and in his late forties, who seemed to be looking for something. On March 2, 1948, a DC3 airliner burst into flames and crashed on the runway, killing 22 passengers, mainly businessmen.

As rescue workers searched the wreckage, they were accosted by a bowler-hatted man concerned as to the whereabouts of his briefcase.

Horseman of Bottlebush Down

Ghosts and spirits have come back across hundreds of years. But none have come further than the mystery horseman who rides the north Dorset countryside.

The horseman of Bottlebush Down is thought to date back to the Bronze Age, which makes him and his mount around 2,500 years old.

His appearances are nearly always close to the A3081 road which runs between Cranborne and Sixpenny Handley in Britain's beautiful West Country. Although the area is today mainly quiet and devoted to agriculture, it was thought to have been a hive of activity thousands of years ago.

The fields are dotted with low, round burial mounds. A strange earthwork, known locally as the Cursus, runs for some six miles across the fields. It consists of two parallel ditches about 80 yards apart and it is here that the horseman is usually seen.

The horseman's ghostly rides have become legend in this part of the West Country. Farmworkers and shepherds have reported seeing him galloping across the fields towards the Cursus and in one incident in the 1920s two young girls were terrified as they cycled one night from Handley to Cranborne.

The wide-eyed girls told police that they were cycling along the road when suddenly a horseman appeared from nowhere and rode alongside them for some distance before disappearing.

But it was a few years earlier that the most documented sighting was made, and the one that put the time stamp on the horseman.

Archaeologist R C Clay had such a close encounter with the rider that he was able to date the apparition by his clothes. Clay, leader of a team excavating a Bronze Age settlement near Christchurch, in Dorset, came face to face with the horseman in 1924 as he was driving home from the excavations to Salisbury, in Wiltshire.

As he passed the spot where an old Roman road crossed the modern highway, he saw a horseman galloping across the fields ahead of him. The horseman was riding full tilt towards the road, but as Clay slowed down to let him cross, the rider swung his horse round and galloped parallel with the vehicle some 40 yards away.

For about 100 yards or more, the horseman kept pace with the car while Clay watched fascinated. In spite of his surprise, the archaeologist managed to take in a great deal of detail about horse and rider.

He said later, "The horse was smallish with a long tail and mane. It had neither bridle nor stirrups. The rider had bare legs, a long flowing cloak and was holding some sort of weapon over his head."

As suddenly as he had appeared, the horseman disappeared. Clay stopped his car and tried to gather his thoughts. His first instinct was to get out and look round, but as it was getting dark he decided to press on home.

The next morning he was back to see if he could discover anything which would help explain his ghostly encounter of the previous evening. He searched the road and the surrounding area for several hundred yards on either side of the spot but found nothing – except a low burial mound almost exactly where the horseman disappeared.

For weeks afterwards he tried to find an explanation for what he saw. He drove along the section of road at the same time, evening after evening to see if in the gathering dusk he might have mistaken an overhanging tree or bank or anything for his galloping horseman. There was nothing.

His one encounter with the horseman, coupled with his expert knowledge, enabled him to date the figure as from the late Bronze Age – somewhere between 700 and 600 BC.

The pilots' pact
'Reunion' of dead airmen

A disused British aerodrome on the flat, empty wastes of East Anglia has not heard the roar of aircraft engines since World War Two. Yet the aura of those days is still there, in ghostly form.

Bircham Newton, in Norfolk, was a Royal Air Force aerodrome that survived two world wars. It was built in 1914, and in recent years has served as a base for students taking building trades courses.

A film team visited the old aerodrome to make a management training film and went to work in what had once been the officers' mess. Suddenly and without apparent cause, a heavy studio lamp fell towards the head of Peter Clark, a member of the film crew. As it was about to hit him, it swerved as if pulled by some unseen hand and crashed across a table.

On its own, this incident would have prompted little comment, but with the events that followed it is more significant.

GHOSTS

Just behind the old officers' mess are two squash courts, built just before World War Two. It was here that another member of the film unit had a terrifying experience. After discovering the old courts, he borrowed a racket and ball and the only key to the building. He asked if any of his colleagues wanted to join him. No one was interested, so he set off to play on his own.

The two courts were side-by-side. At first the film man practised on the left hand court then, for no particular reason, he moved to the other court. While knocking the ball around, he heard footsteps along the viewing gallery behind him.

At first he paid no attention, assuming that one of the film crew had come to watch him play. Then he remembered that he had locked himself into the building and was completely alone.

For a moment he remained silent. Then he heard a sigh which made the hairs on his neck prickle – and turning round saw a man in RAF uniform staring at him from the gallery. Suddenly the figure vanished. The film man fled.

Later he confided in Peter Clark who suggested that they return to the squash court that night and try to record the footsteps on the crew's tape recorder.

Clark explained, "It was a calm warm summer night when we returned to the courts. We visited the left court which felt completely normal, but when we went into the court on the right the atmosphere was so cold, so frightening that it was like stepping into another world."

The two men switched on the tape recorder and waited, but eventually fear got the better of them and they decided to lock the machine in the court and come back when the tape had run out.

What they discovered when they replayed the tape was extraordinary. They heard the sounds of aircraft, voices and clanking machinery – uncannily like the noises of a busy aircraft hanger in wartime. Even more disturbing was a strange, unearthly, groaning.

The tape was analysed by a BBC engineer who admitted that he and his colleagues were perplexed. There was no technical fault with the machine; few outside noises could have penetrated the nine-inch brick wall, and the tape was brand new, so old recordings could not have come through.

The mystery of the tape absorbed Peter Clark. He persuaded friends to return to the aerodrome with a medium and hold a seance. As soon as the medium entered the courts he went into a trance and began to speak in the voice of a dead airman.

Clark described the scene. "It was extraordinary. The medium's face became twisted and he seemed to have difficulty in breathing. He said his name was Wiley".

Spectral Spitfire

People living near the famous Battle of Britain airfield at Biggin Hill, Kent, have often reported the sound of a wartime Spitfire returning from a sortie. Occasionally the plane has actually been seen, screaming low towards the landing strip, then turning into a victory roll.

Further east, at Hawkinge, near Folkestone, villagers have heard a flying bomb – more than three decades after the Germans last launched one at Britain.

Clark discovered in local records that there had indeed been an airman called Wiley, who had committed suicide at the aerodrome during World War Two.

Inquiries also revealed that the aerodrome had been haunted for years. A student attending one of the construction courses had his bedclothes pulled off him at night by an invisible being. Another had his curtains torn down and thrown across the room. And a senior engineer claimed that he had been tapped on the shoulder three times while working alone in the attic of the officers' mess. The experience so unnerved him that he refused to work there again.

One man claimed that he saw a figure in RAF uniform walk through a solid wall which had been built since the war. He was so frightened he refused to complete his course and left the following day.

Some of the psychic recordings were broadcast by the BBC and afterwards many listeners wrote in complaining that their pets had been disturbed by the noises.

A BBC television team decided to investigate and arrived at the aerodrome with two leading spiritualists.

Unaware of the details of the tapes or the hauntings, the spiritualists first entered the left squash court and declared it normal. As soon as they entered the right-hand court they excitedly claimed that it held "a presence", the ghost of a dead airman.

One of the spiritualists, the famous medium John Sutton, began to meditate. He immediately became entranced by the dead airman and spoke as a man called Dusty Miller who had been killed with his friends Pat Sullivan and Gerry Arnold.

When Sutton came out of the trance, he was able to explain that the three airmen had been keen squash players. They made a pact that if anything should ever happen to them, they would try to meet up again in the building. They had all been killed when their plane crashed behind a church which had a tower, but no steeple. He had never been to the area before so could not describe the exact location.

Sutton also explained, "People who die suddenly do not always realise they are dead and so do not understand when they cannot communicate with the living."

He said the three airmen had been held earthbound at Bircham Newton because they had no idea that the crash had killed them. He put the occurrences down to the spirits trying to contact people because they desperately needed help. Having contacted the dead airmen, the spiritualists were able to lay them to rest by a simple exorcism.

After checking records, investigators found that a plane had indeed crashed behind Bircham church during the war, killing the crew of three.

The church has a tower, but no steeple.

The grief of Henry Watts

At the edge of a quiet Wiltshire road stands a small stone cross. Travellers hurrying along the road, between Marlborough and Hungerford, could be excused if they missed the tiny memorial to the 14-year-old boy who died tragically at the spot just over a century ago.

Grass and country flowers almost hide the cross, on which are inscribed the simple words "A H P Watts, May 12, 1879."

But four people driving home from the cinema on a quiet autumn night in 1956 will never forget the memorial. For they came face to face with the grieving ghost of the boy's father.

Little Alfie Watts worked for a carter in the village of Axford, and it was here in 1879 that he met his death. Alfie and the carter were at the head of a team of three horses which suddenly bolted. The man and the lad ran alongside the heavily-laden cart, struggling to halt the runaway team. But as the cart clattered through a steep-sided cutting, Alfie was thrown to the ground.

The boy fell beneath the wheels and died of his injuries two hours later. Mourning villagers erected a memorial to him at that spot.

Years passed and memories dimmed. Occasionally someone remembered the stone cross, and the brambles and grass were cleared away. Then, in October 1956, Frederick Moss and three friends were driving home from the movies to Marlborough when the headlights picked out a tall, thin, clean-shaven man standing in the middle of the road.

He was dressed in a long brown coat and stood with his back to where the cross was almost hidden in the grass.

As the car swept on he made no attempt to get out of the way. Moss blew his horn, but still the figure stayed where it was. It did not even look up.

The driver slammed on the brakes and stopped a few yards short of the figure, but as he got out to investigate, it disappeared.

Moss and his friends searched the area with torches, but found nothing. With the cutting walls rising steeply nine feet on either side, it was impossible for anyone to have climbed up without being seen.

When Moss arrived home shaken, he told his wife what he had seen. As she heard the full description of the mystery man, something clicked in her memory.

She was a native of the area and was born about 20 years after the accident. She said she clearly remembered the boy's father, Henry Pounds Watts, who died in 1907. He was a tall, thin man who dressed in a long brown coat and, unusually for those times, had neither beard nor whiskers.

The Mosses were in no doubt that this was the man on the road – a road which at that time was due to be widened, destroying the little cross. Perhaps Henry wanted to make sure that someone remembered his son's modest memorial before the road was widened.

If that was his aim, it succeeded. The road was widened but the cross was lovingly replaced nearby.

Dead man's quest for justice

A row in Britain's House of Commons during the First World War may have been responsible for the mysterious reappearance of a long-dead pilot. The flier returned to haunt an airbase – three years after the crash that killed him.

Member of Parliament Pemberton Billing, head of the Southampton company which later developed the Spitfire aircraft, accused the Government in 1916 of doing nothing while certain Royal Flying Corps men were "murdered rather than killed by the carelessness, incompetence or ignorance of their senior officers or of the technical side of the service".

One of the examples he cited was that of Desmond Arthur, an Irish Lieutenant with No 2 Squadron, who died in a crash over the Scottish airbase of Montrose on May 27, 1913. Arthur was gliding down from 4,000 feet, preparing to land, when the starboard wing of his BE2 biplane folded in mid-air. As the tiny aircraft plunged, the pilot's seatbelt snapped, and he was thrown out of the cockpit. Ground staff watched him fall to his death, arms and legs flailing helplessly. There were no parachutes in 1913.

The Royal Aero Club's accidents investigation committee began a probe immediately, and concluded that an unauthorised repair job on the plane's right wing had been botched, then covered up. Someone had broken a wing span near the tip, repaired it with a crude splice, then concealed the work by stretching new fabric over the affected area. To Arthur's friends in the Royal Flying Corps, it added up to murder, but the offender could not be pinpointed.

Billing used the Aero Club's findings as a basis for his 1916 onslaught in Parliament. He was as astonished as anyone when the Government, anxious to avoid any scandal that might undermine public faith in its war effort, issued its own report on the crash. It said the wing repair explanation was based on the evidence of only one of 23 witnesses, and was completely without foundation. In other words, Arthur had only himself to blame for his death.

The interim report was issued on August 3, 1916, and a detailed version was promised before Christmas. In September, airmen based at Montrose began to notice curious things. Twice one officer followed a figure in full flying kit towards the mess, only to see him vanish before reaching the door. A flying instructor woke one night to find a strange man sitting in a chair beside the fire in his bedroom. When he challenged the intruder, the chair was suddenly empty. Two other men woke simultaneously one night, convinced a third person was in their room.

Destination death

A coroner's court was told in 1936 that a driver died because he saw the ghost of a London bus. The man's car careered into a wall at the junction of Cambridge Gardens and St Marks Road in North Kensington. And a witness swore that the driver swerved to avoid a General Omnibus which was ablaze with lights – but had no driver or conductor.

Residents in the area said they had frequently seen and heard the phantom No 7 bus racing down Cambridge Gardens in the early hours of the morning. It usually vanished at the junction where the death crash happened. A bus inspector told the coroner he had seen the bus pull into his depot and vanish.

Shortly after the inquest, the wall which had claimed the driver's life was demolished under a road-widening scheme to make the junction safer. The eerie bus has not been seen since.

Was Desmond Arthur trying to rally his old friends in the Royal Flying Corps to clear his name? As the story of the hauntings spread around Britain's other airbases, two of the Government's committee of inquiry revealed that they had not even seen the Royal Aero Club findings that their interim report had denigrated.

After studying the results of the earlier investigation, Sir Charles Bright, an engineer, and a lawyer called Butcher added an amendment to the final report when it was issued that Christmas.

They declared, "It appears probable that the machine had been damaged accidentally, and that the man (or men) responsible for the damage had repaired it as best he (or they) could to evade detection and punishment."

The ghost of the dead pilot appeared to settle for that as vindication of his innocence in causing the crash. After one last appearance in January 1917, phantom flier Desmond Arthur was never seen again.

The headless cyclist

George Dobbs was determined that the bitter weather and shortages of wartime Britain were not going to get him down. It was 1940 and the country was in the grip of one of its worst winters for years. Snow covered the countryside and, to make matters worse, the war news was gloomy.

George wrapped himself up against the hostile night and set out from his home near Northampton to walk to the Fox and Hounds pub for a few beers to cheer himself up.

With his hands deep in his pockets, he struggled up the slippery slope past the cemetery when he noticed the dim headlights of a car slowly approaching, its wheels running in and out of the icy ruts. Framed against the lights of the car, George saw a cyclist pedalling towards him. He too was having difficulty in steering his machine because of the snow and ice.

At first George thought that the cyclist had no head, but he quickly dismissed the idea as being a trick of the light or the fact that the rider had muffled himself up against the cold.

The next time George glanced up, the cyclist was still fighting for control of his machine, completely unaware of the approaching car. But before George had a chance to cry out, the car drew level with him and chugged past towards Market Harborough.

George could not believe it. The car must have hit the cyclist, he thought.
He ran through the snow as fast as he could to the spot where he had last
seen the cyclist – expecting to find the result of a terrible accident.

There was nothing. No cyclist, no cycle and no accident. George searched
both sides of the road in vain.

He fled as quick as his legs could take him to the Fox and Hounds pub at
nearby Kingsthorpe. As he thawed out in the pub, he told his story.

When George finished there was silence – until Lid Green, who was for
many years the local gravedigger, leaned across the bar.

He said, "That sounds just like the chap I buried 25 years ago. He was
knocked off his bike in deep snow outside the cemetery gates.

"His head was torn off in the crash."

Spirit of the disused aerodrome

A young collector of military souvenirs knew who to blame when he
found his tailor's dummy in SS uniform hurled from its regular place
in the hall of his home.

Only days earlier, both the man and his wife had been given the shock of
their lives when an RAF pilot, complete with World War Two leather jacket,
helmet and oxygen mask, appeared in their home in Croydon, south London.
Clearly the ghost did not appreciate finding reminders of an enemy in his
new haunt.

The young couple asked to remain anonymous when in 1978, after a series
of odd happenings, they called in the Society for Psychic Research.

They told investigator Brian Nisbet that the pilot had appeared four times,
first in the wife's bedroom as she prepared for a dinner party, then in the
lounge as the husband watched TV, and twice more in the bedroom, once
when the wife was ironing, once when the couple were together.

After that, they saw him no more – but his invisible spirit began playing
tricks on them and their guests. First he hurled the offending tailor's dummy
ten feet across the hall. Then he turned up in the spare bedroom, where a
young married couple were staying there as guests. In the middle of the
night, the man got up to go to the bathroom. While he was away, the wife
suddenly felt the bedclothes being wrenched from her naked body.

Driving force

A rector of the Yorkshire parish of Wombwell had a ghost which drove itself and the cleric up the wall.

The Reverend David Warner had left his car parked in his driveway with the handbrake on. He said: "The key wasn't in the ignition, but it switched itself on and moved off.

"If it acts as if possessed again, I shall have to exorcise it."

It was the last straw for their hosts – they called in a local clergyman. Even during the exorcism ceremony, the phantom flier could not resist a prank. The wife felt the strap of her bra being plucked, though nobody was standing near her.

Investigator Nisbet discovered that the couple's house was on an estate built on the site of the old Croydon airport.

But he said, "I have not been able to explain any of the things that have happened to these people."

Phantoms of the highways

The hiker, the jaywalker and the hunchbacked postman

The darts match ended early for Roy Fulton. It had not been a lively night. A pint and a half of lager and not much company in the little pub at Leighton Buzzard. Roy, 26, decided to drive to another pub, The Glider, nearer his home, at Dunstable, Bedfordshire.

It was a dark night and foggy patches hung over the flat, open countryside. Roy started up and drove his little van towards the village of Stanbridge. As he neared the first houses, the headlights picked out the dark figure of a youth standing at the roadside, thumbing a lift.

Roy pulled up past the young man and waited for him to catch up. He looked up at a stranger's face. It was pale and drawn and framed by short, dark, curly hair. The young man was probably about 20. The only unusual thing about him was the white shirt he was wearing with an old-fashioned round collar.

GHOSTS

Roy opened the door. The young man said nothing. "I'm going into Dunstable, where are you for?" Roy asked. The young man pointed towards Totternoe, a village beyond Stanbridge. He got in and shut the passenger door. Roy passed Stanbridge and drove on down the Totternoe road at a steady 45 miles an hour. The hitch-hiker sat silently. As the road neared Totternoe, it was lit by streetlights. Roy slowed down and took a cigarette pack from his pocket. "Cigarette?" he asked, flipping open the packet and holding it out to his passenger. There was no reply. Roy shook the packet and turned to his companion . . .

There was no one there. The passenger seat was empty. Roy slammed on the brakes and looked all around him. He stared through the side window at the road stretching into the empty darkness.

A cold draught blew across his neck and a chill gripped his stomach. His left hand edged across to the passenger seat. It was warm.

Roy reasoned that the hiker could not possibly have got out of the car at the speed of 45 mph. And, even if he had, he would have had to open the door and that would have automatically switched on the courtesy light, but no light had come on, and the passenger door was firmly shut.

Shaken, Roy drove on to The Glider. He ordered a large scotch and downed it in one gulp. Ashen-faced, he said, "I've just seen a ghost."

Lorry-driver Laurie Newman spotted what looked like the figure of a nun walking beside the A4 as he drove from Chippenham to Bath at 2.30 one morning. He slowed down to pull out and pass her, but as he did so, the figure turned and sprang, clutching the side of his cab, and leering through the side window. Shocked, Laurie stared back . . . into the face of a grinning skull.

Sebastian Cliffe also experienced a highway haunting as he drove from Bath to Warminster. As he approached a bend at Limpley Stoke, all his dashboard gauges stopped functioning and he felt a sudden chill. Then a ghostly face appeared at his windscreen. As it slowly faded, the gauges began to work again.

Spooky jay-walkers have startled drivers in the West Country. An old gipsy woman staggers across the Bath to Bradford-on-Avon road at Sally-in-the-Wood, a spot notorious for vehicles plunging off the road. And at Barrow Gurney, on the A38 south west of Bristol, several drivers have skidded to a halt to avoid a woman in a white coat who suddenly appears, and then vanishes.

Police at Frome, Somerset, report that at least three motorists say they have been victims of a phantom hitch-hiker. The man, aged between 30 and 40, and wearing a check sports jacket, stops cars between the villages of Nunney and Critchill, and asks to be dropped at Nunney Catch. But when the cars reach the village he has disappeared. One driver was so shocked, he needed hospital treatment.

Has the ghost of a hunchback postman who died in 1899 returned as a 20th century killer? That was one theory being investigated by police in East Anglia after three people died on a lonely country road.

The first victim on the A12 between Great Yarmouth, Norfolk, and Lowestoft, Suffolk, was a lorry-driver who knew the route well. For no apparent reason, his vehicle careered off the road and smashed into trees in 1960. The coroner recorded an open verdict.

Twenty years later a car driver who was also familiar with the road drove crazily into the trees. Within a year, a cyclist unaccountably swerved into the path of a car.

Survivors of accidents on the same stretch of road have also claimed that a "shadowy figure" forced them to swerve. Andrew Cutajar, aged 19, of Lowestoft, said, "The spectre of an old man was standing in the slow lane, just looking at me. I slammed on the brakes and skidded, expecting a thud. The car went straight through him and hit the kerb."

There was no sign of the old man when Andrew got out to investigate.

Former policeman Frank Colby, also of Lowestoft, claims he has seen a hunchback figure with long straggly hair on the A12. "He just walked across the carriageway and disappeared," he said.

Psychic researcher Ivan Bunn, of nearby Oulton Broad, believes the figure may be the ghost of William Balls, a postman whose body was found in the area during the winter of 1899. Could it be that he is still trying to deliver a message ... about his own death?

Chapter Six

Ghosts of Royals and Rulers

Our rulers are the people who shape the living world
– the kings, queens, presidents and prime ministers
whose deeds, decisions and declarations will be
recorded in the history books. Yet many of them
swear they share the corridors of power with men
and women who are already in those books – the
ghosts of their long-dead predecessors ...

The royal haunted house guests

The British Royal Family are well aware of the truth of the old saying, "Uneasy lies the head that wears the crown". For the troubled spirits of their predecessors still haunt the historic royal homes. The Queen, Princess Margaret and the Queen Mother have come face-to-face with ghosts.

Windsor Castle, the royal retreat in Berkshire, is said to have at least 25 different spectral skeletons in its cupboards, four of them former monarchs. It was there that Princess Margaret saw the figure of Queen Elizabeth I, the last Tudor monarch, who has wandered the 12th century building since her death in 1603. She is spotted most frequently in the castle library. An officer of the guard once followed her into the room, but when he reached the door, Good Queen Bess had vanished.

King Charles I, who lost his head in 1649 during the Civil War, has been reported many times standing by a table in the library, while George III, who died on January 29, 1820, and was confined to the castle during the last years of his lunacy, has been seen and heard in several rooms, often muttering one of his most-used phrases, "What, what?"

The bulky figure of Henry VIII is another nocturnal visitor. Two guards saw him fade into a wall on the battlements as recently as 1977. They later learned that there had been a door at that very spot during Henry's reign.

Soldiers on sentry duty at Windsor have often seen the ghost of a young guardsman who killed himself in 1927. Many who have spotted him in the Long Walk believe at first that he has come to relieve them.

A Coldstream Guardsman found unconscious in the Great Park in 1976 had experienced a very different kind of ghost. He told those who found him that he had seen Herne the Hunter, a man clad in deer skins and a helmet with antlers jutting from the forehead.

Hundreds of other people claim to have seen the same apparition over the last 250 years, silently speeding through the castle grounds with his spooky pack of hounds. When the tree from which he allegedly hanged himself was cut down in 1863, Queen Victoria reserved the oak logs for her own fire, "to help kill the ghost". But the sightings of Richard II's forester have continued.

In the 17th century, a terrified servant called Parker approached one of the castle guests, Sir George Villiers, with an extraordinary story. He said he had had three visits from the armour-clad ghost of Sir George's father, the Duke of Buckingham, and had been told that unless Sir George mended his callous ways, he had not long to live. Sir George laughed off the warning. Six months later he was assassinated.

Hampton Court, the palace by the Thames presented to Henry VIII by his disgraced Chancellor, Cardinal Thomas Wolsey, is still haunted by the spirit of the King's fifth wife, Catherine Howard, who was beheaded in 1542. She has been seen so frequently, running screaming to the chapel door in search of sanctuary, that she is now mentioned in the official guide issued to the thousands of tourists who visit the palace.

The third of Henry's six wives, Jane Seymour, has also been seen at Hampton long after her death. She emerges from the Queen's apartments carrying a lighted taper, and walks around the Silver Stick Gallery on the anniversary of the birth of her son, later Edward VI, on October 12, 1537. Jane died one week later, and the weakling boy, crowned for a short reign when he was only ten years old, was fostered by a nurse, Mistress Sibell Penn, who also appears at Hampton.

Mistress Penn was buried at St Mary's Church after she died of smallpox in 1568, but the church had to be rebuilt in 1829 after being struck by lightning. The nurse's remains were disturbed as her tomb was moved, and soon strange whirring sounds and mutterings were heard coming from behind a wall at the palace where there was no known room.

When the wall was knocked down, a spinning wheel was uncovered along with other relics which indicated that the nurse had once lived on the site. Many witnesses have also seen Mistress Penn wandering the corridors of the palace's south-west wing, where her old room was. She is a tall, thin hooded figure in a grey robe, her arms outstretched as if in appeal. In 1881, a sentry watched her walk through a wall.

Two male figures once haunted Hampton's Fountain Court, making loud noises in the middle of the night. The ghosts were never seen or heard again after workmen uncovered two skeletons in Cavalier dress buried beneath the courtyard. The skeletons were given a Christian funeral.

Perhaps the most bizarre Hampton phantoms were those encountered by a police constable on duty at the palace one cold February night in 1917. The officer, identified only as PC 2657, who had 20 years service in the force, opened a gate in the grounds for two men and seven women wearing strange old-fashioned costumes. He swore that they then walked on for 30 yards, turned to one side of the path – and simply faded away.

Today the Queen and her immediate family have abandoned Hampton Court to the tourists, and divide their time in Britain, between Buckingham Palace, Windsor, Sandringham in Norfolk, and Balmoral in Scotland. All have their own curious ghosts.

Windsor Castle, Berkshire, England.

Clock Court, Hampton Court Palace.

Hampton Court Palace,
Hampton Court, London.

Glamis Castle, Scotland.

These are some of the historic homes owned by the British Royal Family and said to be haunted. Glamis Castle above is central to Shakespeare's *Macbeth*. Hampton Court is also famous for its maze. Queen Elizabeth II is frequently at home at Windor.

GHOSTS

It was at Balmoral that the Queen is said to have seen the phantom figure of John Brown, confidant and some say lover of the widowed Queen Victoria. He has often been reported stalking the castle's corridors and entrance hall, a magnificent sight in his kilt.

Sandringham has for years played host to a mischievous yuletide poltergeist. It livens up Christmas Eve in the second floor servants' quarters by flinging greetings cards about, ripping sheets from newly-made beds, and breathing heavily in the ears of unsuspecting maids. Prince Philip's uncle, Prince Christopher of Greece, once saw a mysterious masked woman while staying in one of the Sandringham guest rooms. He glanced up from his book and saw her head and shoulders framed in the dressing table mirror. She had soft, curly brown hair, a dimpled chin, and a mask over the top of her face.

Next day, while visiting Lord Cholmondely at nearby Houghton Hall, the Prince found out who she was. He saw a portrait of the same woman, carrying a mask, and wearing the dress he had noted in his mirror. It was Dorothy Walpole, unhappily married in the 18th century, whose ghost was also seen by King George IV in 1786.

The ghost of Buckingham Palace is that of Major John Gwynne, a private secretary in the household of King Edward VII early this century. Fearing that mention of his name in a divorce case had brought dishonour on the Royal Family, he shot himself at the desk of his first-floor office. And it is there that his dim shape has been seen several times since.

Gatcombe, the Cotswolds mansion home of Princess Anne and Captain Mark Phillips, is said by locals to be haunted by a huge black dog. They call it the Hound of Odin, named after the God of the Vikings who pillaged Gloucestershire 1,000 years ago, and was always accompanied by a fierce four-legged fiend.

Kensington Palace has three ghosts. A man in white buckskin breeches strolls the arcaded courtyards, Queen Victoria's Aunt Sophia sits working a spinning wheel, and, on the roof, King George II has been seen staring at the weather vane, and asking, in his thick German accent, "Why don't they come?" The King died at the palace on October 25, 1760, waiting for messengers with news from his native Hanover.

No ghostly goings-on have yet been reported from the Gloucestershire home of Prince Charles and Princess Diana, but St Paul's Cathedral in London, where they were married in July, 1981, was once the scene of a strange incident. Workmen preparing foundations for a building beside it unearthed a wooden box containing jewels. The gems were taken to the British Museum, London, and an expert took them home to clean, polish and value.

As he and his daughter worked, the room suddenly grew cold. A psychic

Corpse in the bed

A gruesome ghost haunts St James's Palace in London – the figure of a man propped up in bed with his jaw hanging open over a gashed throat. It has been seen frequently since the night of May 31, 1810, when Sellis, the Italian-born valet of Ernest Augustus, Duke of Cumberland and fifth son of King George III, was discovered dead on his bed.

The Duke told the inquest that, when he returned from a night at the opera, Sellis had tried to kill him, failed, and committed suicide. He denied later gossip that he had murdered his valet because he was being blackmailed after seducing the man's daughter.

friend who called a few hours later found out why. He saw a tall thin man in Elizabethan dress standing behind the couple, clearly angry that his hidden treasures had been disturbed.

There was another surprise when the jewels were put on display at the museum. A woman looking at them suddenly fainted, and explained after attendants revived her, that she had seen blood on one of the necklaces. Staff could find no trace of stains on the gems, but the woman remained convinced that the person who last wore the necklace had been murdered.

Of all the hauntings connected with royal buildings, the most intriguing are those of Glamis Castle. The towered and turretted fortress beside Dean Water, near Forfar, Angus, is the Scottish family home of the Queen Mother's family, the Bowes Lyons. Princess Margaret was born there. But its 16-feet thick walls have been cloaked with mystery ever since Macbeth usurped the Scottish throne by murdering King Duncan in one of the rooms in the year 1040.

The Queen Mother delights in telling the younger members of her daughters' families the spine-chilling tales that have sprung up about Glamis. How Lord Beardie Crawford and fellow revellers diced with the devil in a tower room, and were condemned to stay there, drinking eternally until the Day of Judgement. Of how the Ogilvies, fleeing from the Lindsays during a clan war, were locked in a room and forgotten, starving to death.

The Queen Mother herself is one of many who have seen the sad Grey Lady of Glamis, who haunts the Clock Tower. She is believed to be the ghost of Janet Douglas, wife of the sixth Lord Glamis, who was burned to death on Castle Hill, Edinburgh, in 1537 after being falsely accused of witchcraft and of plotting to poison King James V.

There is one Glamis phantom that few in the family have ever been prepared to talk about. Victorian high society was alive with rumours that a hideously mishapen beast of a man had been born into the Strathmore clan, an immensely strong and hairy egg-shaped creature whose head ran straight into a hugh body which was supported by toy-like legs and arms.

Unable to reveal the monster's existence, yet unable to kill it, the family were said to have locked their odd offspring in one of the secret rooms built at Glamis in the last years of the 17th century. There it lived for years, known only to the Earl of Strathmore, his lawyer and land agent, and, when he reached 21, the Earl's heir.

Guests returned from Glamis with strange stories that fuelled the gossip. Many said they had been woken in the night by the howls and snarls of an animal. One woman claimed she saw a pale face with huge, mournful eyes staring at her from a window across a courtyard. When it disappeared, she heard appalling screams, and watched an old woman scurry across the yard carrying a large bundle.

In 1869, a Mrs Monro woke in her bedroom at the castle to feel a beard brush her face. As she fumbled for a light, the shape that had been standing over her shambled into the next room, where her son was sleeping. The boy's screams of terror brought Mrs Monro and her husband racing to his bedside. As he explained that he had just seen a giant, they all heard a crash.

At breakfast next morning, other guests said they too had heard the crash, and one said she had been woken by the mournful whines of her small dog. But their hosts could offer no explanation.

In 1865, a workman who found a secret passage, and claimed to have seen something alive in a room off it, was "subsidised and induced to emigrate".

In 1877, essayist Augustus Hare watched the Bishop of Brechin offer to share the burden that was making the then Earl of Strathmore morose at a house party. Hare reported, "Lord Strathmore said that in his most unfortunate position, no one could ever help him."

Andrew Ralston, land agent to the Strathmores from 1860 to 1912, was once asked for the full story by the Countess, grandmother of Queen Elizabeth II. He replied, "Lady Strathmore, it is fortunate you do not know it, for if you did you would never be happy."

Dowager Lady Granville, the Queen Mother's sister once admitted, "We were never allowed to talk about it when we were children. Our parents forbade us ever to discuss the matter or ask any questions about it. My father and grandfather refused absolutely to discuss it."

And the 12th Earl, the Queen's great-grandfather, was quoted as saying, "If you could only guess the nature of the secret, you would go down on your knees and thank God it was not yours."

His warning failed to deter historians and ghost-hunters. For years they tried to unravel the nature of the secret. Once, towels were flown from the window of every known room, to try to locate the possible hideaways. Experts combed the family tree for clues, and in the 1920s journalist Paul Bloomfield came up with what seemed a plausible explanation.

According to Burke's Peerage the "bible" of British nobility, Lord Glamis, heir to Thomas, the 11th Earl of Strathmore, married Charlotte Grimstead on December 21, 1820, and was presented with an heir, Thomas George, later the 12th Earl, on September 22, 1822. But when Bloomfield checked Douglas's Scots Peerage, he surmised that Lord Glamis and his wife also had a son "born and died on October 21, 1821." Another reference book gave the date as October 18.

Bloomfield guessed that the first-born son did not die, but was badly deformed. He could never inherit the title and estates. Expected to live only days, he was kept alive and well cared for, but he survived both his father and his younger brother. A third son, Claude, became the 13th Earl, and was succeeded in 1904 by his own boy, Claude George, born in 1855 and who became father of the Queen Mother.

It is believed that he was the last heir to be initiated into the grim family secret, when he reached the age of 21 on March 14, 1876. His son and successor, Timothy, was never told the story, although he once said, "I feel sure there is a corpse or a coffin bricked up in the castle walls somewhere, but they are so thick that you could search for a week without finding anything."

Today, the legend of the monster lives on only in the name of the rooftop lead path where he may have been exercised at night – the Mad Earl's Walk.

The Grey Lady still prays silently in the chapel. Spirits still haunt the room where the Strathmore's personal hangman used to sleep. And Earl Beardie is still seen, a huge old man with a flowing beard, sitting by a fire in one of the castle bedrooms.

Yet for all their ghosts, none of the royal palaces and castles rank as the most haunted place in Britain. That title rests with an ancient fortification that kings and queens of earlier ages used for less civilised purposes ...

Long live the dead King!

The ghost of King George IV stalks the underground passages of Brighton Pavilion, the place he loved most.

He built the Sussex landmark after secretly marrying Mrs Fitzherbert while he was Prince Regent. His spectre has been encountered both in the passage that leads to the stables – now the Dome – and in a tunnel which once linked the royal cellars with those of the Druid's Head Inn.

The Pavilion was sold to the town of Brighton by Queen Victoria, for £50,000.

The Bloody Tower

History of horror goes back 700 years

The Tower of London's ancient battlements, colourful Beefeaters and legendary ravens attract millions of tourists each year from all over the world. They stroll the picturesque buildings and courtyards, and listen enthralled as guides bring to life the spectacular and violent happenings that shaped Britain's past. For the Tower was once the most blood-drenched spot in England, and for more than 700 years it has had the ghosts to prove it.

The first, in 1241, was that of Saint Thomas Becket, who had been murdered at Canterbury Cathedral 71 years earlier. Becket was a Londoner, and had been Constable of the Tower before becoming Archbishop of Canterbury in 1162. His spirit was seen by "a certain priest, a wise and holy man". It was said to have returned to demolish extension walls which were upsetting people who lived near the Tower. The priest saw the apparition strike the walls with a cross, whereupon they fell as if hit by an earthquake.

Later Tower ghosts had more personal reasons for returning to the London landmark. Anne Boleyn, the second of Henry VIII's six wives, is the most frequently seen spirit. Several sentries have spotted her over the years, and one even faced a court-martial because of her.

He was found unconscious outside the King's House on a winter's night in 1864, and accused of falling asleep on watch. At the hearing, he told how a strange white figure had emerged from the dawn mist. It wore a curious bonnet which appeared to be empty. The private, who served with the King's Royal Rifle Corps, challenged the figure three times, but it continued to move towards him. When he ran the bayonet of his rifle through the body, a flash of fire ran up the barrel and he passed out.

Two other soldiers and an officer told the court-martial they had seen the apparition from a window of the nearby Bloody Tower. After hearing that the incident had taken place just below the room where Anne Boleyn spent the night before her execution for adultery on May 19, 1536, the court-martial cleared the unfortunate sentry.

Anne, Queen for 1,000 days, had a horror of English steel in English hands, and her husband agreed to import a French executioner with a French sword for the beheading. But after her death, there were no more niceties. Her headless body was bundled into an old arrow chest and buried in unseemly haste in the Tower chapel of St Peter ad Vincular.

The Traitor's Gate at the Tower of London.

GHOSTS

Sentries have often seen her ghost pacing up and down outside the tiny church, and one night, one of the guards noted an eerie light shining from inside the chapel. He climbed a ladder to peer through a window, and saw a ghostly procession of knights and ladies in Tudor dress file slowly up the aisle, led by a woman who looked like Anne. When she reached the altar, they all vanished, leaving the chapel in darkness again.

Anne's restless spirit does not confine itself to the scene of her death. Her headless body is said to arrive in a phantom coach at her childhood home, Blickling Hall, Norfolk, on the anniversary of her execution, and she has also been reported wandering through the grounds and attics of Rochford Hall, Essex, during the 12 days after Christmas.

But it is at the Tower where most of her rambles have taken place, often near the time of other executions. At 2 am on February, 1915, Sergeant William Nicholls and his watch saw a woman in a brown dress with a neck ruff. She walked quickly towards the Thames, which runs past one side of the Tower, then disappeared into a stone wall. Five hours later, a German spy was shot in the moat, one of 11 executed there during World War One. Anne was last seen in February, 1933, when a guard reported a headless apparition floating towards him close to the Bloody Tower.

The ghosts of three other 16th century ladies who lost their heads have also been spotted in the Tower. Catherine Howard, the fifth of Henry VIII's wives, was beheaded there in 1542, and has been seen walking the walls at night. Margaret, Countess of Salisbury, re-enacts the horrors of her 1541 execution on its anniversary. She was dragged screaming to the block, and the axeman chased her round the scaffold, missing his target three times before finally severing her head. Lady Jane Grey, who reigned as Queen for only nine days, has been reported several times.

Two sentries recognised her when they saw the figure of a woman running along the battlements of the inner wall, near the Salt Tower, at 3 am on February 12, 1954 – the 400th anniversary of her beheading on Tower Green, less than 150 yards away. Exactly three years later, two Welsh Guardsmen spotted a white shapeless form on the Salt Tower, where Lady Jane was imprisoned before her execution, at the age of 17.

In 1970, a man from Grays, in Essex, wrote to a London evening newspaper, saying his girlfriend had seen what seemed to be a ghost during a visit to the Tower. He said the figure of a long-haired woman, wearing a long black velvet dress and white cap, was standing by an open window in the Bloody Tower. A large gold medallion hung round her neck. The girl was the only one in her party to see the figure, and she said that, when she went up to the window, both on the visit and on a later occasion, she found it difficult to breathe. Experts believe she is one of the very few people who have seen Lady

Jane Grey in daylight.

Phantom men and children also roam the Tower. In 1890, a sentry described an encounter so vivid that he "Nearly died of fright." He was on duty in the Beauchamp Tower when he heard someone call his name.

He said, "I turned and there, floating in mid-air, was a face, red and bloated, with a loose, dribbling mouth and heavy-lidded pale eyes. I had often seen it in the history books – it was Henry VIII, with all the devil showing in him.

"I was so scared I did not stop running until I came upon two of my comrades. They were beginning to clamour, when they suddenly broke off – the face had followed me.

"The affair was hushed up, and we were all told not to breathe a word that the Tower was haunted."

During World War One, another sentry reported seeing a ghostly procession pass him near Spur Tower. A party of men were carrying a stretcher bearing the headless corpse of a man, his head tucked in beside his arm. Historians said this was the practice in earlier centuries, when bodies were returned to the Tower for burial after executions on Tower Hill.

Boadicea's return

Some of the oldest names in Britain's history books have emerged from the mists of time to appear as ghosts more than 1,000 years after their deaths. The warrior queen Boadicea poisoned herself in AD 62 to avoid capture after her army was routed by the Romans.

But on some mornings earlier this century, she was seen at the small village of Cammeringham, north of Lincoln, with two phantom horses pulling the chariot from which her hair and gown billowed behind her. The village is close to the old Roman Road, Ermine Street.

When the Romans withdrew from East Anglia in AD 410, Ella was crowned the region's king. And the people of Horning, near Norfolk, say his ghostly coronation is re-enacted every five years on July 21 beside the river Bure.

The boy-king Edward was murdered by his stepmother, Queen Elfrida, in AD 979, and his body taken to Shaftesbury Abbey, in Dorset, for burial. So many miracles happened while it was being transported that the boy later became St Edward the Martyr. Several people claim to have seen him being carried up cobbled Gold Hill in Shaftesbury by two ghostly men leading phantom packhorses.

At Tamworth Castle, Staffordshire, the figure of Editha, grand-daughter of King Alfred the Great, has been sighted climbing the stairs to the Tower Room, wearing her black nun's habit. Her sighs and moans have been captured on a tape-recorder.

GHOSTS

The ghost of a former Duke of Northumberland has been seen so often on the battlements between the Martin and Constable towers that sentries have nicknamed the pathway Northumberland's Walk. Sir Walter Raleigh, the favourite explorer of Elizabeth I, who was imprisoned in the Tower by her successor, James I, and executed in 1618, has also been reported by guards; and two little children seen walking the Bloody Tower hand-in-hand are believed to be Edward and Richard, the two princes allegedly murdered on the orders of their uncle in 1483, so he could claim the throne as King Richard III.

Some of the Tower's many ghosts are not recognisable as personalities. The Keeper of the Jewel House, Major-General H D W Sitwell, woke one morning in 1952 in his quarters in St Thomas's Tower, on the outer wall, to see a monk in a brown habit through the open door of his bedroom.

Some of the ghosts are not even human. In October 1817, Edmund Swifte, then Keeper of the Crown Jewels, was dining with his wife, son and sister-in-law in his parlour in Martin Tower. As he offered his wife a glass of wine, she exclaimed, "Good God, what's that?"

He followed her startled gaze, and saw a cylindrical glass tube, about as thick as a man's arm, and filled with white and blue liquid which seemed to be constantly churning. It hovered between the top of the table and the ceiling, moving slowly from one person to another until it passed behind Swifte's wife, pausing over her right shoulder. She crouched and clutched her shoulder, shouting, "Oh Christ, it has seized me." Swifte lashed out at the cylinder with a chair, then rushed upstairs to check that the couple's other children were all right. When he returned, the apparition had vanished.

Only days later, a sentry outside Martin Tower watched vapour pour through the narrow gap between the closed door and sill, and take the shape of a giant bear. The guard lunged at it with his bayonet, but the cold steel passed through the figure and stuck in the wooden door. The man collapsed from shock, and never recovered. When Swifte visited him the following day, he declared him "changed beyond recognition". Within days, the sentry was dead.

The Tower also has its share of mischievous spirits. Several Yeoman Warders have found themselves bundled out of bed in one particular small bedroom in the Well Tower. In the autumn of 1972, a photographer was sent tumbling from a ladder as he set up his camera to take pictures of a mural in the Beauchamp Tower room where Lord Lovat, the last Tower prisoner to lose his head, had been held.

Perhaps the most curious fact about the Tower of London hauntings is that none have ever been reported in the White Tower, the largest and oldest of all the buildings, and the heart of the entire complex. Guy Fawkes, the man who tried to blow up the Houses of Parliament in 1605, was just one of the celebrities incarcerated there in cruel conditions before his gruesome death – but none have ever returned to the scene of their ordeals.

Masons restoring one of the walls in the late 1850s may have uncovered a clue to the reason for that. In the 11th century, when work on the White Tower began, it was believed that buildings could be protected against malevolent spirits by sacrificing an animal in them. Eight centuries later, the repair men broke into one of the thickest stone walls ... and found the skeleton of an ancient cat.

The tragic Queens

The ghosts of two tragic Queen Marys still haunt the houses where both found temporary respite from their unhappy lives in the 16th century. Both were Catholics caught on the wrong side of the power struggle in England following the death of Henry VIII.

Mary Tudor, Henry's elder daughter, was staying at Sawston Hall, near Cambridge, when her weakling brother, Edward VI, died. Before the news reached her, the powerful Duke of Northumberland tried to stage a coup. He seized the Tower of London, proclaimed his daughter-in-law, Lady Jane Grey, queen, and sent his men north to capture Mary.

She was asleep in the Tapestry Room at Sawston when her host John Huddleston learned of the approaching danger in the early hours of July 8, 1553. He woke her, and smuggled her out of the hall's back door disguised as a milkmaid. From a nearby hilltop, she reined in her horse to watch the Duke's frustrated soldiers set fire to Sawston.

After she became Queen on July 19, Mary showed her gratitude to the Huddleston family by helping them to build an even finer hall, which was completed in 1584. Since her death in 1558, Mary has often been seen there in the Tapestry Room, which survived the fire, or walking majestically in the grounds. Sometimes the haunting strains of the virginal she used to play there for her father have been heard.

Mary Stuart, Queen of Scots, spent years as a captive in English mansions and fortresses before Queen Elizabeth I had her executed at Fotheringhay Castle on February 8, 1587. She was moved from home to home, the unwitting focus of attention for every Catholic plotter with a grudge against the Protestant Good Queen Bess, and her ghost has been reported in many of the places that were her prisons.

She has also been seen in places with happier memories. When she was held at Fotheringhay, she used to attend mass undetected by visiting Southwick Hall, three miles away, via an underground tunnel. Her spirit has been sighted there since her death.

In 1878, a guest at Nappa Hall, Wensleydale, Yorkshire, claimed he had met a "very lovely ghost" whom he recognised from portraits as Mary. She was tall, slim and wearing a black velvet gown. Mary visited the hall while under arrest at nearby Castle Bolton.

Beaulieu, Hampshire, was the scene of one of Mary's escapes from her long years in captivity. Even today, ghostly footsteps are heard rushing down the Palace House staircase she used for her freedom dash.

The most curious story concerning Mary Stuart came after her son King James VI of Scotland and later James I of England, ordered that Fotheringhay, where his mother had died, be destroyed.

Many of the fittings from inside its stone walls were bought by a local innkeeper, William Whitwell – including the oak staircase by which Mary reached her room. Whitwell later installed them in his inn, now The Talbot at Oundle, Northamptonshire, and found to his dismay that a phantom was part of his purchase.

The ghost of Mary, Queen of Scots.

Curse of Civil War

Uneasy lie the bones of the Crown's enemies

The greatest crimes against nature, according to Church and government teaching in bygone centuries, were killing a king and waging civil war. Both happened in Britain more than 300 years ago, when Oliver Cromwell's Roundheads defeated the Royalist Cavalier armies, and beheaded King Charles I. Ghostly echoes of that catastrophic conflict have lingered around the country ever since.

Edge Hill, on the border between the counties of Warwickshire and Northamptonshire, was the scene of one of the bloodiest battles. More than 40,000 fighting men clashed there on Sunday, October 23, 1642, as Prince Rupert led the King's troops into action against Cromwell's Parliamentarians. At the end of the day, the fields were littered with dead and dying, and

Fight for the Standard at the Battle of Edge Hill.

both sides withdrew to continue the war elsewhere.

The following Christmas Eve, a group of shepherds were hurrying home at around midnight when they passed the battlefield. The sound of approaching drums, the clatter of arms, and the awful groans and screams of dying men stopped them in their tracks. Before they could take to their heels, the rival armies materialised all around them, eerily-lit colours blowing in the wind as they blazed away at each other with muskets and cannon. The bizarre action continued for more than three hours, finally fading at just after 3 am on Christmas morning.

When it was all over, the bemused shepherds ran to the nearby village of Keinton, and woke the local justice of the peace, a man called Wood, and the local minister, a Mr Marshall. Both swore an oath that the men were not drunk, and agreed to accompany them to Edge Hill the following night. News spread quickly during the day, and when darkness fell, the crowd included "all the substantial inhabitants of that and neighbouring parishes".

They were not disappointed. The two armies "appeared in the same tumultuous warlike manner, fighting with as much spite and spleen as formerly". Terrified spectators arrived home in the early hours to pray for deliverance from what they believed to be a hellish visitation. For a week, it seemed their prayers had been answered, but the following Saturday night, the horrifying scenes of bloodshed and cruelty were re-enacted, "with far greater tumult", for four hours.

Eventually, rumours of the phantom battles reached King Charles in Oxford. He sent three officers and three other "gentlemen of credit" to investigate the stories. Mr Wood and Mr Marshall led them to Edge Hill, and they saw for themselves the gory action replay. The officers had seen the fighting on the actual day of the battle, and recognised many of the spectral clashes – even the faces of some of the combatants. The King was convinced. He declared that the nightmare tableau was a sign of God's wrath against those who waged civil war.

Over the years, the sounds and sights of war have been reported many times by people passing Edge Hill, although the fighting has never been as vivid as it was that first Christmas.

Three years after Edge Hill, Cromwell's forces routed a Royalist army at Naseby, Northamptonshire, and for nearly 100 years, generations of villagers from miles around gathered at the site on the anniversary of the battle to watch it re-enacted in the skies, and listen to the din of the guns, and the groans of the victims. With time, the phenomenon faded, but the echos of a third civil war battle continue to this day.

A Royalist army of 4,000 was slain at Marston Moor, Yorkshire, during another Roundhead victory on July 2, 1644, and drivers travelling through the area have seen groups of dazed, bewildered men in Cavalier clothing staggering along by the roadside as if trying to escape pursuers. Two motorists who saw them in 1932 described vividly the long cloaks, high boots, long hair and wide-brimmed hats with cockades, typical of Royalist dress of the period.

The ghosts of the two leaders of the rival armies have also been seen since their deaths. King Charles was beheaded in 1649 at Westminster, and his body taken to Windsor for burial. It has been seen in the castle library there. He is also said to be the headless phantom of Marple Hall, in Cheshire.

Cromwell's spectre has been reported both at the Golden Lion at St Ives, Huntingdon, his regional headquarters, and walking in Red Lion Square, London, with two ghostly aides, John Bradshaw and General Ireton. The bodies of the three men were said to have been exhumed and carted there, on their way to Tyburn jail, after the Restoration of King Charles II in 1660.

Cromwell's most dramatic reappearance came in the winter of 1832. England was again seething with revolt because of a controversial Reform Bill, and an angry mob was besieging Apsley House, the London home of the Duke of Wellington. As the Duke paced his room, deeply troubled over what line he should take when the Bill was debated, he met an armour-clad figure he recognised from portraits as that of Cromwell.

The phantom did not speak, but pointed meaningfully at the crowds outside the house. Long after the Bill was passed, Wellington revealed that he had seen the ghost – and that it had changed his attitude to the reforms.

A ghost also changed the mind of an army leader during the civil war. The Duke of Newcastle had occupied Bolling Hall at Bradford, Yorkshire, on behalf of the King, and ordered that everyone in the Parliamentary stronghold be executed at dawn next day. His soldiers were puzzled when he withdrew the order shortly before they were due to carry it out. They learned that a female figure in white had appeared by their leader's bed three times in the night, wringing her hands and pleading, "Pity poor Bradford".

Forty years after the war England was again in the grip of internercine fighting. The Duke of Monmouth led a rebellion against James II, but his

---

Legions of the lost

In 1887, a British officer took a holiday in the Thuringian Forest in what is now East Germany – and saw a Roman legion march past him as he sat by the roadside. He found later that he was on the site of a battle between the Romans and a German tribe 2,000 years earlier.

GHOSTS

West Country army was crushed in the last battle fought on English soil, at Sedgemoor, Somerset, on July 6, 1685. The ghosts of some of the 1,000 men slaughtered have since been seen at the site of their deaths, and a phantom Cavalier horseman is said to be the Duke himself. He escaped capture at the battle, but was beheaded nine days later.

A cruel sequel to the bloodshed was witnessed by a group of schoolchildren walking up Marlpit's Hill, near Honiton, Devon, in 1904. They saw a wild-looking man in a black wide-brimmed hat and a long, brown coat. His dazed look troubled the children, though their teacher saw nothing.

Research showed that the bedraggled ghost may have been that of a man who had escaped the carnage of Sedgemoor, and made his way back to his wife and children, who lived in a cottage on the Hill. As he neared his front door, a troop of soldiers rode up, and cut him down with their swords.

Monmouth supporters who survived the fighting were tried by Judge George Jeffreys in a series of cases which became known as the Bloody Assizes. Slavery, transportation, flogging and execution were the sentences he meted out in a legal reign of terror. Since then, his ghost, complete with black cap used to deliver death sentences, has been seen in rooms where he stayed during his West Country tour of duty – at Clough's Hotel, Chard, Taunton Castle, the Great House, Lyme Regis, and Lydford Castle.

The American Civil War, which lasted from 1861 to 1865, has also left phantom reminders for future generations. One of the most horrific battles was at Shiloh, where 20,000 men died. Next day, locals reported that a nearby river ran red with blood. And the sights and sounds of the battle have been re-enacted in the skies over the battlefield.

Wars between nations hae also left their mark on the supernatural world. The eerie footsteps of marching knights in armour have been heard at the historic English West Country site of Glastonbury, and headless war horses have been seen galloping through a Wiltshire valley near Woodmanton, the scene of an ancient battle between the Britons and the invading Romans.

In 1745, more than 30 Cumbrians watched a phantom army march through the sky above Souter Fell at the time of the Jacobite rebellion, and ghostly soldiers have been spotted at the site of the 1746 Battle of Culloden in Scotland.

During World War One, soldiers from both the German and Allied armies told tales of supernatural intervention in the fighting of August 26, 1914.

The British Expeditionary Force had taken a battering and looked like being over-run by the Kaiser's troops. Then the so-called Angels of Mons

---

Sceptics beware!

If you don't believe in ghosts, keep your opinion to yourself when you visit the Kings Arms Inn at Monkton Farleigh, Somerset.

In 1974, one of the customers poured scorn on the idea of such things, and his words were followed by a loud crash upstairs, then a flood of water through the ceiling.

A heavy freezer being defrosted had been pushed forward on to its face. On another occasion, a tray of steaks was thrown across the room after doubts about ghosts were expressed.

The pub also has several inexplicable sounds. Several people have heard an old woman talking to children in one room, manager Eric Muspratt heard heavy boots walking along an upstairs corridor in the early hours, and several regulars have heard the flapping wings of a large bird in the bar. Each time, the room has suddenly become icy cold.

---

appeared, causing consternation in the German trenches. The British had time to retreat and regroup.

Author Arthur Machen, who wrote a story for the London *Evening News*, described the angels as phantom bowmen from the 1415 Battle of Agincourt. But he later claimed that he had made the whole thing up. The paper was deluged with letters from officers and men saying they had seen the spectres.

An officer from Bristol told his story in a local church parish magazine. He said his company had been cut off by German cavalry, and he expected certain death. Then the angels appeared between the two forces, and the German horses were terrified into flight. A brigadier general and two of his officers told the same story to their chaplain. And a lieutenant-colonel claimed that, during the retreat, phantom horsemen guarded his cavalry battalion for 20 minutes, escorting their flanks in fields by the road.

After the war, it was learned that both German and French troops involved in the Mons bloodshed had seen unearthly allies helping the British. Cynics argued that the three armies were exhausted by heavy fighting, and could have been hallucinating. By then the Angels of Mons had served their purpose. Morale in the British trenches after the battle was sky-high.

On August 4, 1951, two English women on holiday in the French town of Dieppe awoke to the sound of gunfire. For three hours they made a note of every sound, and experts who examined their record found it a carbon copy of what had happened on August 19, 1942, when more than half a 6,000 strong Anglo-Canadian force was wiped out trying to storm the German-held Normandy port in a dawn raid.

The women asked fellow guests at their hotel about the sounds but no one else had heard a thing.

Hail to the dead chief
Shawnee curse puts paid to Presidents

Abraham Lincoln is still in the White House in Washington, but he is far from alive and well. For the President who led the United States out of the bitter Civil War, only to be assassinated by a fanatic in April, 1865, now haunts the corridors of power as a ghost. American leaders and other celebrated visitors all claim to have seen him or felt his presence over the last 100 years.

Sir Winston Churchill, Britain's wartime Prime Minister, did not enjoy sleeping in Lincoln's old bedroom, and frequently moved to another room across the hall during the night. Queen Wilhemina of the Netherlands is said to have fainted after answering a knock on the Rose Room door to find Lincoln standing outside. And President Theodore Roosevelt once said, "I see Lincoln – shambling, homely, with his sad, strong, deeply-furrowed face – in different rooms and halls."

It was in 1934, during the presidency of Franklin Roosevelt, that Lincoln made his most dramatic appearance. Mary Eben, one of the White House staff, entered a bedroom on the second floor to find a figure in an old-fashioned black coat sitting on the bed and pulling on a pair of boots. She stared, stunned, at the man for several seconds before he vanished.

More than 40 years earlier, another White House aide made a public appeal to Lincoln's ghost to leave him alone. John Kenney was personal bodyguard to President Benjamin Harrison between 1889 and 1893, and his nerves were frayed by footsteps in corridors and rapping on doors which seemed to have no natural explanation.

On a visit to Baltimore, he attended a seance, at which Lincoln's spirit was present. Kenney is said to have said, "Please don't do it again, Mr Lincoln. I am guarding the life of President Harrison now, and you've got me so scared I can't do my duty."

Kenney never heard the ghost again.

Lincoln is said to step up his visits to his old offices in times of crisis. The chief White House usher saw him several times during World War Two, and one of Theodore Roosevelt's valets fled shrieking from the building. President Eisenhower said he sensed Lincoln's presence many times.

Even while Lincoln was alive in the White House, as the 16th President of the United States, there were ghosts there. His wife, a confirmed spiritualist, saw her brother Alexander after he was killed while fighting on the

The ghost train

President Abraham Lincoln was shot dead in 1865 by John Wilkes Booth in a Washington theatre. His coffin was carried on a special funeral train, which stopped for eight minutes at each station along the route so people could pay their respects.

Soon afterwards there were reports of a phantom train. It was draped in black and bore the President's coffin. One carriage carried a band of skeletal musicians. As the ghostly train passed along the funeral route, clocks stopped.

For exactly eight minutes.

Stairway to terror

The quick tempers of successive owners of a mansion at Sutton, Surrey, produced two ghosts on its staircase. In 1713, a messenger from gout-ridden Queen Anne of England arrived at Carshalton House to ask her physician, Dr John Radcliffe, to travel to court immediately.

The doctor flatly refused, and when the envoy tried to change his mind, he flung the man down the stairs, breaking his neck.

Dr Radcliffe died before he could be tried, and the house was bought by Sir John Fellowes. Only a few years later, he had a heated argument with a tax collector on the first floor landing – and the revenue man plunged to his death after being knocked over the balustrade.

Afterwards, the ghosts of both victims were regularly seen on the staircase.

Confederate side in the Civil War.

Lincoln himself had a vision of his own death. He told an aide shortly before his assassination that he had been woken by quiet sobbing.

He said, "I wandered downstairs until I came to the East Room. Before me was a catafalque with a corpse whose face was covered. 'Who is dead?' I demanded of the mourners. 'The President,' was the reply. 'He was killed by an assassin.'"

Franklin Roosevelt's death in 1945 came in chilling circumstances, and many lay it at the door of an ancient Shawnee curse.

What is known as the Indian's Revenge started nearly 180 years ago when Shawnee chief Tecumseh died in a pitched battle with William Harrison, then Governor of Indiana.

In revenge, the Shawnee placed a curse on Harrison. Medicine men told how the Governor would become president in a year ending in zero – but would die in office. From then on, any President elected in a year divisible by 20 would also die before his term ended.

Harrison – grandfather of Benjamin – was duly elected president in 1840 – and died a month after taking office.

Abe Lincoln was elected 20 years later – and was assassinated.

The deaths of five other presidents have also been attributed to the Shawnee curse . . .

James Garfield was elected to office in 1880 and was assassinated in 1881.

William McKinley was re-elected in 1900 and was assassinated in 1901.

Warren Harding was elected in 1920 and died of a stroke in 1923.

Franklin Roosevelt was elected in 1940 and died in 1945.

John Kennedy was elected in 1960 and was assassinated in 1963.

White lady of Bohemia

Tiny Petr Vok was a very special baby. He was born in 1539, the sole heir and last in the line of the aristocratic Rozmberk family of South Bohemia. His father, Josta, was desperate that nothing should stop him continuing a lineage that stretched back for centuries.

He hired a team of nannies to maintain a 24-hour watch on the boy at his home, Krumlov Castle, on the banks of the river Vltava. They were with him constantly, caring for him by day, sleeping in his room at night.

One night, one of the nannies woke with a start. The room was strangely bright, glowing with moonlight. As she stared round it, she saw a curious, misty figure beside Petr's cradle. Speechless and shaking with fright, she watched the intruder, a woman in white, gaze down at the sleeping child. As the babe started to cry, the woman gently picked him up, cuddled and stroked him, kissed him, and tenderly placed him back in the crib. Then she disappeared.

Still shaking, the startled nanny woke her colleague, and told her what she had seen. Gingerly, they crept to the cradle. Little Petr was sleeping peacefully, a smile between his pink cheeks.

The two nannies had heard the legend of the White Lady, a ghost said to haunt the castles of the Rozmberk family. They had dismissed it as folklore. Next night, they both stayed awake to see if the woman returned. The room was locked, the windows shut, but just after midnight they saw a pale light, and the phantom nanny appeared again. She rocked the cradle, caressed the child, then, seemingly satisfied that all was well, dissolved into a wall.

Each successive night, the two girls waited for the White Lady to appear. She never let them down. Content that she meant no harm, they took her for granted, and did not bother to stay awake. Then one of the regular nannies fell ill, and a temporary replacement moved in. Nobody told her about the White Lady, and as she lay tossing and turning, unable to sleep, she saw the ghost arrive at her usual time. Next morning, she told one of the other girls what she had seen, and was told, "Don't worry, the White Lady takes care of Petr at night."

But the girl was worried. What would the master say if something happened to the boy? How could she explain that she had left him in the care of a ghost?

Next night, she again lay sleepless as the phantom appeared, walked to the cradle, and rocked it. When Petr started to cry, she picked him up. Then the anxious nanny leapt from her bed, and walked bravely to the figure.

Engraving by George Cruikshank of *Herne the Hunter appearing to Henry VIII on the terrace of Windsor Castle.*

She grabbed the child from her arms. The White Lady put up no resistance. She stood motionless, then turned to the girl and said sternly, "Do you know what you are doing, bold one? I am a relative of this newborn child, and it is my right to be with him. You will not see me here any more." The ghost made a cross sign on the wall, then disappeared into it.

Petr grew up to inherit the castle when his father died. He was told the story of his mystery guardian, and often discussed her with friends and relatives. One day he decided to check the wall where she had last been seen. Workmen began knocking a hole – and discovered a cache of coins and gems.

Who was the caring White Lady? There are two theories. An historian believed she was Lady Perchta, a Rozmberk who married an aristocrat called Jan Lichtenstein. But he proved cruel and merciless, and eventually she left him and his selfish family, and fled to Krumlov. Later she moved to Vienna, to live with her daughter, and died there in 1476. A portrait of her and her husband still hangs in the castle at Jindrichuv Hradce in South Bohemia, today part of Czechoslovakia.

Another theory is that the White Lady is Marketa, daughter of the Archduke Maidburce. She married Jindrich, from the Hradce castle family, but when he died in 1362, became a recluse at a convent in Krumlov. From time to time she visited her children and friends, wearing an all-white nun's habit.

Whoever she was, there are many documented sightings of her in the homes of the Bohemian nobles. Apart from Krumlov, she was seen in castles at Telci, Bechyn, Trebon and Jindrichuv Hradce. The accounts of her are always the same: a woman of breeding, all in white, with a hood over her head. She was seen just before anything happy or sad was to happen – if the news was bad, she wore black gloves instead of white.

Workmen renovating part of the Jindrichuv Hradce castle once spotted

---

Vision of the Abbess

When the Abbess of Laycock told friends that she had seen her son William Longespee in her rooms one night in 1250, they found it hard to believe.

For William had left England to join a Crusade in the Holy Land, and was not expected home for at least another year.

But the Abbess said she recognised him from the insignia on the shield of an eerie skeleton-like knight who had appeared before her. Six months later a messenger arrived from Egypt.

Longespee had been hacked to death by Saracens on the day of the apparition.

her at midday, at a window in a tower. They were startled, because no one had been in the tower for years and the staircase had been destroyed by fire. They watched her for some time before she slowly faded from sight, as if moving across the room.

Servants at the castle often saw her in the corridors at night, sometimes with a bunch of keys hanging at her waist. Her face was always serious, but never frightening. As she flowed along landings, opening doors, some servants spoke to her. She would answer with a movement of her head or hand, or even with a few words.

The servants believed she was taking care of the families to whom she was related, looking after the young, warning the adults of danger, and preparing the dying for their fate.

In 1604, one of the Hradce family, a man called Jachym, fell suddenly ill, but nobody thought his condition could be fatal. Then, on a cold, snowy January night, a priest at the castle woke with a start, and thought he heard someone calling him. Dressing hurriedly, he opened his door and found a woman in white.

"Do not waste any time," she said in an urgent voice. "Follow me." The priest turned back to look for a light, but the woman took his lantern, breathed on the glass, and a flame flared up.

She led the way to the castle chapel, where the astonished priest found candles burning everywhere, as if in readiness for a Mass. The woman told him to collect everything he needed to perform the last rites. Still puzzled, he did as she directed, then followed her to Jachym's bedroom door.

Here both she and the light vanished, but by now the priest realised who she was. He went into the bedroom, and found the servants asleep. On the sickbed, Jachym was clearly gravely ill and fighting for his life. The priest performed the last rites, and the master, the last of the Hradce line, died in peace.

The caring nature of the ghost points to her being Marketa, as Sedlacek suggested. She was once supervising renovations to part of Jindrichuv Hradce castle, and to encourage the workmen, she promised them all sweet pudding when they had finished – and every year after that.

When the work was complete, by the late autumn, Marketa kept her promise, and prepared a great feast. But as the men and their families sat down at long tables in the castle courtyard, snow began to fall on to the sweet pudding.

The following year, the hostess switched the date of the feast to early spring, and the tradition of feeding the poor on "Green Thursday" continued throughout her lifetime, and the lives of her successors, long into the 16th century.

This is the most famous of medium Einer Nielsen's seance photographs, and shows Queen Astrid of Denmark as she is supposed to have materialised. Queen Astrid was killed in a car crash at Lucerne in 1935. Her subsequent appearances at Nielsen's Copenhagen seances were often witnessed. The photograph was taken by Liljeblad, who wrote a book, in defiance of Church authorities, testifying to the authenticity of the Queen's materilisation. Many sitters were present when this picture was taken. Liljeblad used three cameras, taking his pictures simultaneously with a white flash. All the people present saw the materialisation and the medium together.

Phantom bride

A lady dressed in brown has haunted Raynham Hall, a magnificent mansion near Fakenham, Norfolk, for more than 250 years. She has been seen by a king, shot at by a famous author – and even captured by a camera.

The lady is believed to be Dorothy Walpole, sister of Sir Robert Walpole, who became Britain's Prime Minister in 1721. And her unhappy spirit is said to return because of a tragic love life.

Dorothy's father, also a member of Parliament, and also called Robert, became guardian to a young viscount, Charles Townshend, when the lad was 13. As he and Dorothy grew up together, they fell in love, but they were denied permission to marry. Dorothy's father feared people would think the Walpoles were after the Townshend fortunes.

Charles left to find consolation in the arms of a baron's daughter, and later married her. Dorothy drifted first to London, then Paris, drowning her sorrows in a reckless whirl of parties, and eventually scandalising high society by setting up home with a rakish French lord.

Then, in 1711, news reached her that Charles's wife had died. She hurried home to Raynham, and 12 months later the childhood lovers were married. For a while they were blissfully happy. Then the bride's past caught up with her. Her husband was told of how she had lived in Paris. In a rage, he confined her to her rooms, and ordered the servants to let no-one in – or out.

When Dorothy died, aged 40, ten years later, in 1726 the official cause was given as smallpox. But local rumour said she has been pushed from behind at the top of the hall's great staircase. Such gossip gained credence when servants from Raynham revealed that her ghost was soon seen wandering the corridors of her old home.

In 1786, the Prince Regent – later to become King George IV – was a guest at the hall. He woke one night to find a woman wearing brown standing beside his bed. Her hair was dishevelled, her face ashen white. The royal visitor fled the room in his nightgown and nightcap, and stormed through the house, rousing everyone with his wrath. He refused to stay an hour longer.

Alarmed at upsetting such an honoured guest, the Townshends ordered a nightly watch by servants and gamekeepers. A few nights later, the patrols sighted the lady in brown. But when one of the men moved into her path to challenge her, she walked straight through him. He felt an icy cloud pass into his bones and out again.

The brown-clad spectre cut short Christmas merrymaking at Raynham in 1835. Several guests left early after seeing her. Colonel Loftus, brother of the then Lady Townshend, bumped into her on consecutive nights. He described her as a stately woman in a rich brocade dress and a cap. Her face was clearly defined, but she had black hollows instead of eyes.

Dorothy's fame spread. Captain Frederick Marryat, the tough, sea-going author of *Mr Midshipman Easy* and *The Children Of The New Forest*, was invited to meet her for himself when he scoffed at the ghost stories. When he arrived at the hall, he was given a room where a portrait of Dorothy hung. It helped him recognise her late that night when he and two friends spotted her walking towards them down a corridor. They darted into a side room, but the lady stopped opposite the door, and gave then a wicked grin. Marryat was holding his pistol, and fired a shot at the shape. It went straight through the still-smiling spectre and smashed into the wooden door behind.

In 1936, two professional photographers arrived at Raynham Hall to take pictures of the house for Lady Townshend. On the afternoon of 19 September they were setting up their cameras at the foot of the staircase when one of them saw what seemed to be a cloud of vapour taking human shape. He shouted instructions to his colleague, who exposed the photographic plate without knowing why. When it was developed, the misty outline of a woman in a white gown and veil could be seen halfway down the stairs, and experts were convinced the picture was not a fake.

Had Dorothy Walpole decided to let the world see what she looked like on her wedding day 224 years earlier – on the steps where, some say, she was pushed to her death?

Chapter Seven

Ghostly Friends and Lovers

Hauntings do not have to be horrific.
Understandable initial terror among those who
confront the unknown can sometimes be replaced by
gratitude, even friendship, once humans realise that
the spooky spectres they have encountered mean no
harm – and are even anxious to help. Stars of the
stage and screen are among those who have
discovered that inexplicable apparitions can be
amiable, affectionate – and even amorous.

The spooky chess player

Maurice Tillet was grotesquely deformed. A gentle giant, he was a professional wrestler with the soul of a poet. Highly intelligent, he could speak 14 languages.

Tillett died in 1955. Yet 25 years later American businessman Patrick Kelly claimed to have regularly played chess with him – from beyond the grave.

Years earlier, he and Kelly had often played chess in the businessman's home near Braintree, Massachusetts. During the game Tillet often raised his terrible head, looked sadly at Kelly and groaned, "How awful it is to be imprisoned in this body."

Kelly said that once his friend Tillet's spirit was free of its heavy burden, he often returned to the chess board "and we play as before".

The ghostly games began after Kelly bought an electronic, computerised chess set. The businessman had always played on his library desk, where a plaster-cast of Tillet's death mask had stood for almost a quarter century.

Late one evening the computer deviated from its programmed plays and used an 18th century opening invented by a French master – a play Tillet had used constantly. Kelly recalled, "I played out the game, and next morning noticed that the computer was not plugged in.

"I thought nothing of it at the time, but a few weeks later the computer suddenly used a similar opening – and again it was not connected to any power supply."

Kelly had electronic engineers check the system. They found the computer would operate without electricity so long as Tillet's death mask was near. Puzzled, the businessman had the mask X-rayed for concealed electronic devices – but it was solid plaster.

According to Kelly the unplugged set would not operate for days at a time, indicating that Tillet's spirit was absent.

Kelly says, "When I want a game, I set up the pieces without plugging the set in. If there is no response I know Maurice is not present. But often in mid-game the computer will play above its normal level, and I know he has stopped by. I prove this by pulling out the plug, but the game still goes on."

Tillet was born in France but in his 20s developed "acromegaly," a horrific disease which causes an uncontrollable growth of the bones.

After coming to the United States, he became a wrestler. He died when he was 45, and Kelly firmly believed that his old friend's poetic spirit was finally allowed to roam free of its grotesque body.

Who haunts ya, baby?

Film stars and the friendly ghosts

...im to have seen ghosts, but few
... that has haunted Telly Savalas.
... TV cop Kojak, was driving home
... ng Island, New York, in the early
... board, he noticed that the clock
... uel gauge registered empty.

... all-night café filtered through the
... asked the way to the nearest gas
... an through the woods at the back
... eway.

... ut when I heard someone ask in a
... rned and saw a guy in a black
... assenger seat and we drove to the

... t – it must have fallen out of my
... insisted I must pay him back and
... a scrap of paper. His name was

... his good samaritan in the phone

167

book. A woman answered the call. Yes, Harry Agannis was her husband. But, no, it was not possible to speak with him, for he had been dead for three years.

The actor's first reaction was shock. He came to the conclusion that there must have been some mistake, but he could not put the incident out of his mind. Eventually, he visited the woman, taking with him the piece of paper on which the stranger had written his name and address.

Savalas said, "When I showed her the paper she was obviously deeply affected and told me that without doubt it was her husband's handwriting. I described the clothes the man had worn. She said those were the same clothes Harry Agannis had been buried in."

The famous actor and the widow sat and looked at each other for a long time, hardly daring to admit to themselves the implications of what had happened. Was Savalas helped by the ghost of Harry Agannis?

He says, "That was a case Kojak could not solve. I doubt if I'll ever be able to explain it."

Screen spectre

Two British film starlets were scared out of their wits when they reported for work at the newly-opened Bushey film studios in Hertfordshire. They saw a luminous blue aristocratic lady stalk across the darkened set. Locals who later saw the spectre recognised her as Lulu, the wife of Baron von Herkomer, whose country mansion once stood on the site of the studios.

Roger Moore, famous as screen master-spy James Bond, admits to being "absolutely petrified" by the experience he had of the supernatural.

Moore had gone to bed early one night after a hard day's filming. He had been sleeping soundly, but suddenly woke up with a feeling that someone was in the room.

He said, "Lying there with the light of the moon coming through the window I saw a misty substance – that's as near as I can describe it – floating across the bed. I was rigid with fright. When it disappeared I looked at my watch and saw that it was precisely 2 am."

The following night he woke at exactly the same time and again saw the strange, drifting mist move across his bed. "I was not keen on going to sleep in that room again, I can tell you. But our home help, a devout Jehovah's Witness, told me to leave a Bible, opened at the Twenty-third Psalm, on my bedside table. Rather reluctantly I agreed to do that and try one more night. It worked and I never had the experience again."

Mystery 'Legionnaire'

A family in Nottingham, central England, fled their home after seeing and hearing strange things during the early 1970s. The man of the house, a lorry-driver, and his daughter, claimed they had seen a man in what seemed to be a Foreign Legion uniform.

Psychic researchers who investigated recorded sudden curious drops in temperature, footsteps, loud screams and hysterical sobbing. Spiritualists at a seance concluded that the mysterious "Legionnaire" was, in fact, the ghost of a young window-cleaner who had killed himself after being left paralysed by a fall from his ladder. The unhappy spirit had fallen in love with the lorry-driver's daughter.

It is surprising how many famous stars live in haunted houses. Some have come to terms with their domestic ghosts, others have fled in search of new property. Peter Sellers' ghost travelled with him. He was always sure that the great comic, Dan Leno, was his guiding spirit through life.

Glenn Ford and his wife Cynthia have experienced strange goings-on in their Hollywood home. Sometimes at night there have been echoes of some long-gone party in their garden. Cynthia Ford says, "There is laughter, as though someone has just told a joke, and the clink of glasses.

"Once when we went downstairs in the morning all the garden furniture had been arranged in a circle. At least its a happy manifestation. Once I even smelled cologne of a type that isn't made any more – the sort that Valentino wore."

Actress Elke Sommer and husband Joe Hyams had no idea when they bought a Beverly Hills house that it was haunted. Soon after they moved in they began to hear strange noises coming from the dining room after they had gone to bed.

Any possibility of burglars or intruders was soon dismissed. The thumping, banging and strange noises went on night after night, always in the same room. Then, in the early hours of one morning when they were both asleep there was a frantic pounding on their bedroom door.

Joe Hyams opened it to find no one there – but thick, black smoke was billowing up the staircase. He rushed downstairs to find the dining room on fire. Elke Sommer sought the advice of several mediums and each one gave the same answer. Whoever the ghost was, it had probably set fire to the dining room as an act of mischief, then repented and decided to warn them.

British actress Adrienne Posta has managed to live with her ghost for years. "He's very friendly," she insists. "The house has such a nice atmosphere I would hate to leave it." Adrienne almost accepts the ghost as part of the family. "Sometimes he gets a bit agitated, then he crashes about and opens and closes doors. That's a nuisance, but not really frightening.

"The only time I got really annoyed was when he persistently threw open my bedroom door in the middle of the night. I was really beginning to suffer from lack of sleep and felt I had to do something about it. So one night I retaliated. I threw a book towards the door when it opened and gave him a piece of my mind. The pestering stopped."

Another star who decided to tackle a household spirit was Chad Everett, famous for his role in the TV saga *Centennial*. His home on Hollywood Boulevard was haunted by a poltergeist. When he and his wife, Shelby, arrived home after an evening out they would be greeted by lights flicking on and off all over the house.

They were not particularly worried by this, but when the ghost became more and more boisterous, throwing things across the kitchen, upsetting furniture and generally making itself a nuisance, Chad decided to take things in hand.

He decided that the only way to tackle the spirit was by treating it like a naughty child.

He said, "One day I just stood in the middle of the kitchen while things were being hurled around and said firmly, 'I think you're a fool to waste so much energy. It is difficult enough to communicate yet here you are wasting your precious energy just frightening us. You're just making yourself miserable. Settle down and don't do it again.' And it didn't."

From that day on, the Everetts lived in peace, though they were always aware of that other presence. The actor says, "I like to think I gave the poor ghost some good advice."

Two stars – Vincent Price and Kim Novak – had startling experiences that lasted only a few seconds but which were never to be forgotten.

Price, master of the macabre, had his extraordinary glimpse of the unknown while flying from Hollywood to New York on November 15, 1958. He was immersed in reading a classic French novel for most of the journey, but at one point glanced idly out of the window. To his horror he saw huge, brilliant letters emblazoned across a cloud bank, spelling out the message TYRONE POWER IS DEAD.

Price admits, "It was a terrific shock. I began to doubt my senses when I realised that nobody else on the plane appeared to have seen them, but for a few seconds they were definitely there, like huge teletype, lit up with blinding light from within the clouds."

Actor Vincent Price, star of many horror movies.

Actress Kim Novak whose eerie experiences on location in Chilham Castle, Kent, England cause her to keep in company.

When Price landed in New York he was told that his close friend, actor Tyrone Power, had died suddenly a couple of hours earlier.

Kim Novak's encounter with the supernatural was just as startling, but alarmingly physical. The lovely blonde actress was working on location in England, making the film *The Amorous Adventures of Moll Flanders* at Chilham Castle in Kent, a 17th century house built round the keep of a Norman castle.

One evening after filming she was relaxing in her room, playing records.

She said, "I put on one of my favourite tunes and couldn't resist dancing to it. As I whirled round the room I suddenly felt rather cold.

"A powerful force seemed to grab me round the waist. I was lifted off my feet and slammed against the wall."

That was all, but it was enough to make Kim turn off the record player and hurry in search of company.

British singing star Cilla Black feels protective towards her ghost. Four times within a period of seven years, she woke up in the night to find the figure of a young girl, no more than 16, standing by the side of her bed.

She said, "When it first happened, in my drowsy state I thought one of the children had come into the bedroom, perhaps wanting a drink of water or upset by a nightmare. The second time, I knew it was a ghost.

"She was so sweet I didn't feel frightened. In fact, believe it or not, I quite liked her being there. She appears to be wearing a long dress, like a nightie and just stands there. She never looks at me.

"I have actually spoken to her, asked her why she has come back and why she can't find peace. But she never answers. She just floats away through the door."

Some famous people have had ghostly experiences in their childhood that have haunted them ever since, staying fresh and vivid in the memory. Actress Stephanie Lawrence, star of the hit London musical *Evita* is one. She says, "When I was a child, our home was an old house on Hayling Island that had once been an army training school. It was full of long corridors and dark corners. One evening I was walking along one of the upstairs corridors when I heard footsteps behind me and what sounded like the patter of dog's paws.

"I spun round quickly and there was a soldier in bright red and gold uniform with a golden labrador by his side. I was absolutely terrified and rushed downstairs to find my brother. I've never forgotten it. I can still see him standing there."

Stephanie discovered that the house had been called "Stonehenge" because a great pile of stones stood in the garden, apparently marking the

---

Kinetic come-back

Richard Lever was puzzled when doors started slamming shut at his TV rental showroom, even when there was no draught. He put it down to the age of his building in the ancient town of Bath.

Then lights started switching themselves off, and television sets changed channels for no reason. "It isn't a control you can set off by radio," he told a reporter in 1975. "It's a push-button control and it takes a lot of force to press it."

Electricians were called in, but could find nothing wrong with the light switches or TV controls. Then Mr Lever was told that a man called Walker, who had lived and died in the house many years earlier, was an energy-saving fanatic with a mania for closing doors and switching off unnecessary lights.

Mr Lever said: "I don't believe in ghosts, but some force here is doing something."

---

spot where a soldier's horse had been buried. Her parents found many army relics under the floorboards, including an old scarlet and gold braid uniform from the time of the Crimean War. She often wonders if it had once been worn by the ghost she saw.

Tiny blonde acress Charlene Titon, who plays the part of Lucy Ewing in the TV series *Dallas*, believes she was haunted by the ghost of her grandfather when she was a child. Even when she became a teenager and eventually left home, the feeling that she was being haunted stayed with her.

As a little girl, she lived with her mother and grandfather in a small modest flat in Hollywood. The old man died and six-year-old Charlene had to be left alone while her mother went out to work. One day, Charlene remembers, her mother returned from work to find her crouched on the front doorstep, shivering with fright. The little girl tearfully explained that there was "somebody scary" in the flat.

Charlene said, "Without hesitation my mother told me that my grandfather's spirit was still there."

Strange things happened as the years went by. No one actually saw the old man's ghost after that but his presence was felt. Charlene said, "I remember very clearly something incredibly scary when I was a teenager. One day a neighbour called in and asked if I would turn down the radio, which was blaring out pop music. In a teenage tantrum I refused.

"Then things began to happen. The plug jerked out of the wall without anyone being near it. When I pushed it back into the socket it was jerked out again so violently that sparks flew. The neighbour stood there with her mouth open, struck dumb by what she had seen, but we knew it was the ghost again."

When Charlene left home to live in another district she thought she had left the disturbed spirit behind. She was determined to think no more about it. She and her boyfriend found a pleasant apartment and settled down there together. But soon the boyfriend began to complain that the place was "spooky".

Charlene agreed. "You could sense something or someone invisible when you walked into an empty room. There were pockets of cold air and nearly every night doors would open silently and close again."

Eventually Charlene could stand it no longer. She moved out, hoping that whatever it was that was haunting her would grow tired of following in her footsteps. She bought a beautiful home of her own in California overlooking a canyon. It seemed to be one move too many for the ghost. If it *was* her grandfather, she believes he has now found peace.

Phantoms of the stage

All the world's a stage for the haunting performances of ghosts, but they seem particularly fond of theatres. Often they are connected with real dramas as strange as any fictional play.

William Terriss was a colourful adventurer turned actor. In December, 1897, he was playing the lead in a thriller called *Secret Service* at the Adelphi Theatre in The Strand. One night, as he left the stage door, he was stabbed to death and ever since his restless spirit has been blamed for a series of inexplicable happenings.

Actors have heard curious tappings, and the sound of footsteps. Mechanical lifts have been moved by invisible forces, and lights mysteriously switched on and off. In 1928, a comedy actress felt the couch in her dressing room lurch under her, as if someone was trying to move it. Then her arm was seized, leaving a bruise. The startled woman had not heard of the ghost until her dresser arrived, and explained that she was using the dressing room which had belonged to Terriss.

The phantom star's strangest performance came in 1955. Jack Hayden, foreman ticket collector at Covent Garden Tube station, noticed a distinguished figure in a grey suit and white gloves who looked as if he was lost. But when Hayden asked if he could help, the man vanished into thin air.

Four days later, the same figure returned and put his hands on the head of 19-year-old porter Victor Locker.

Pictures of Terriss were shown to both men, and they instantly recognised him as their ghost. Both also asked to be transferred. Other London Transport staff on the Piccadilly Line have spoken of a strange presence at Covent Garden, and in 1972 a station-master, signalman and engineer all reported seeing the man in grey.

More than 50 cleaners at London's Drury Lane theatre claim to have seen a phantom wandering the dress circle in a long grey coat. The 18th century dandy in a powdered wig has also been spotted from the stage during rehearsals, and actors regard the sightings as a good omen – they usually herald a successful run for a play. The eerie visitor could be linked with a macabre discovery by workmen in 1860. Inside a hollow brick wall, they found a skeleton with a dagger between its ribs.

A publicity gimmick that backfired introduced actress Judy Carne to the ghost of the Theatre Royal, Bath. A mock seance was arranged to promote her appearance in a production of the Noel Coward play, *Blithe Spirit*. But the light-hearted stunt became serious when the medium hired to host the proceedings started to receive real messages.

Judy, the "sock-it-to-me" star of the TV *Laugh-In* show, said: "We were all absolutely spellbound, including two cynical newspaper reporters. The voice of a woman told us she had been an actress who had starred at the theatre. She had been married, but had fallen in love with someone else.

"Her husband and lover fought a duel, and her lover was killed. Heartbroken, she hanged herself in the dressing room. As I listened, I became very emotional and felt real pain. I tried to talk to her, and ask if she was still unhappy, but the table we were sitting round rattled, and I heard weeping. I often went back to the theatre to try to contact her again, but she never re-appeared."

Could the heartbroken 18th century actress be the phantom lady in grey who haunts the theatre and the buildings on either side of it? She has often been seen by actors, sitting alone in a box. She was there on August 23, 1975, when the curtain went up on a performance of *The Dame Of Sark*, starring Dame Anna Neagle. Theatre staff have also noted a strong smell of jasmine whenever she is near – a scent also familiar to a succession of landlords at the Garrick's Head public house next door.

Bill Loud, Peter Welch and Peter Smith all sniffed it in the cellars during their tenancies, and all also reported tricks by unseen hands – phantom tapping on doors, cuff-links and pound notes disappearing, only to turn up later in rooms where nobody had been for days, candles flying across the bar, cupboard doors rattling, and a fridge being mysteriously switched off.

On the other side of the Theatre Royal is the house once occupied by Regency buck Beau Nash and his last mistress, Juliana Popjoy. Today it is a restaurant called Popjoy's. One would-be diner got more than he bargained for when he called just before Christmas, 1975.

He ordered his meal, then went upstairs to the bar while the dishes were being prepared. As he sat on a green settee, enjoying an aperitif, a lady in old-fashioned clothes approached, sat down beside him, and vanished. The terrified man rushed downstairs, blurted his story to a waiter, and fled, still hungry, into the night.

The jasmine lady may have been responsible for an unexpected drama on the Theatre Royal stage in June, 1963. One of the props for the production was a clock. When its hands reached 12.30, it chimed loudly three times. But stagehands had removed the chime mechanism before the performance began.

A lady in grey also haunts the Theatre Royal in York. Actress Julie Dawn Cole, best known as a nurse in the long-running British TV series *Angels*, is one of many who claim to have seen her. Julie said, "We were rehearsing on stage one Christmas when I saw her wearing a cloak and a hood. Her outline was irridescent, like gossamer, but I was left with a warm, happy feeling. I consider myself lucky to have seen her."

British actress Thora Hird does not have such fond memories of her brush with the supernatural. The popular TV comedy star was appearing on stage in London in a play set in Victorian times. She found a bolero-type jacket in a trunk of theatrical jumble, and at first it seemed ideal for her role, fitting her perfectly, but at each subsequent performance, it grew tighter, until it had to be let out.

Thora said, "One day, my understudy had to wear the jacket. That night,

---

Ghostly barking

Norma Kresgal, of New York, was awakened by the barking of Corky, her collie dog. But Corky was dead. Mrs Kresgal got up to investigate – and found that the house was on fire.

In Wichita, Kansas, Mrs Lowanda Cady was woken by the barking of her dead dog and drove off a thief who had been raiding her kitchen.

Walter Manuel awoke in terror the night he dreamed about his pet dog Lady which had died three weeks earlier. In his dream, Manuel heard the dead pet barking frantically. He awoke and rushed to the bedroom window of his home in a Los Angeles suburb. Outside he saw his two-year-old son, clad in pyjamas, topple into the garden pool. He rushed to the rescue and dragged the child from the water.

at home after the show, she saw the ghost of a young Victorian woman wearing the same jacket. Later, the wife of the director of the play tried the jacket on, and felt nothing. But when she took it off, there were red weals on her throat as if someone had tried to strangle her. We decided to get rid of the jacket.

"A few days after we did, three mediums held a seance on the stage of the theatre. One had a vision of a girl struggling violently with a man who was tearing at her clothes."

The site of a former theatre in Yorkshire is haunted by a woman who did not really exist. Old Mother Riley was a comedy favourite with British film, radio and music hall fans in the Forties and Fifties. She was the creation of comedian Arthur Lucan, who died in his dressing room at the old Tivoli Theatre, Hull, in 1966, a week before he was due to attend a meeting with local tax inspectors.

Ironically, when the theatre was demolished, a tax office was built in its place, and Lucan may be having the last laugh on the staff.

An Inland Revenue official said, "We do not like to say too much about what Old Mother Riley is up to in Hull, but people do stay away from a storeroom on the second floor. There is a strange atmosphere and it is said that the ghost of Mother Riley has been seen."

Matthew's paranormal pal

The ghost who didn't believe in ghosts

One of the most intriguing supernatural mysteries of modern times involves a young Englishman named Matthew Manning.

Matthew was 16 when in 1971 he first came face-to-face with a 300-year-old ghost. It was a meeting which had a profound effect on his life – a life affected by the supernatural, paranormal and bizarre.

Since then he has developed strange psychic powers – such as the ability to bend forks, stop watches and prevent electricity flowing.

But all this was yet to come on the day Matthew saw a shadowy figure on the staircase of his 17th century house in the village of Linton, in Cambridgeshire.

At first, he thought it was a burglar; then he realised it was a ghost. He spoke to the ghost – and the spirit replied. It even remained long enough for

---

Saved by a ghostly comrade

British soldier Gerald Pooler owed his life to a ghostly comrade. Corporal Pooler had left his London home to serve in the Royal Signals Regiment during the Burma campaign of World War Two.

One night he took cover behind a pagoda during a Japanese artillery bombardment. He had decided to get some sleep when a shadow fell across him and he looked up to see a Sikh soldier, who told him that his captain wanted him at once.

When he arrived at the signals office, he was told nobody had called him. Puzzled, he headed back to the pagoda – and found the top of it had been hit by a shell. A chunk of stone weighing a ton was lying on the spot where he had been napping.

Pooler said later: "The astonishing thing was that there were no Sikh soldiers at our HQ. The nearest were 20 miles away."

Matthew to sketch it. This was the start of a long and fascinating association.

Matthew learned that the ghost's name was Robert Webbe and that he was born in the house in 1678. He added the front portion of the house, where he was usually seen, in 1730, and died there about three years later.

Webbe's clothes and wig were of the 1720s style, and he walked with the aid of two sticks, complaining of his "troublesome legs."

Matthew said, "When I first saw him, I thought he was completely solid. He was wearing a green frock coat with frilled cuffs and a cream cravat. He said, 'I must offer you my most humble apology for giving you so much fright, but I must walk for my blessed legs.'

"I grabbed an old envelope and pencil, and sketched him where he stood. A few moments later he turned, walked up the stairs and disappeared."

Some time later, Matthew discovered he had the power of automatic writing: when the writer lets his hand and pen be guided by another mind. In this way, he exchanged many messages with Robert Webbe, and was able to check the historical accuracy of some of the things he was told.

Then Webbe began writing on the walls of Matthew's bedroom, although he was never seen doing it. Over a six-day period in July, 1971, more than 500 pencilled names and dates appeared on the walls. They were in a variety of styles of handwriting and were the names of Webbe, his family and other families who had lived in the area. The majority were from his own lifetime, but there were some from periods ranging from 1355 to 1959.

Matthew was not the only member of his family to be caught up in this supernatural world. His father, architect Derek Manning, told of vividly real sensations he had experienced while lying in bed. He was often awakened by the sensation that someone had climbed into his bed and superimposed another body on his. He even heard the scratching of a man's unshaven chin on the sheets beside him.

Sometimes he felt as though he was "standing in a cage, looking out on to a purple sky, with rocks all round the entrance."

Then it seemed as though he was "in the centre of someone's mouth, looking out through their teeth."

At the same time, he experienced a prickling and tingling in the lower right leg, which eventually spread through both legs – similar to the symptoms of gout. This is almost certainly what pained Robert Webbe and may eventually have caused his death.

The ghost has sometimes played mischievous games on Matthew and his family. Strange antique objects have been found on the stairs. Some of the family's possessions have been spirited away. Things like old prints from the walls, a scarf, and a 50p piece from a money box which was later found abandoned on the stairs.

The bed in Matthew's parents' bedroom has often been found with the covers thrown back, and sometimes the pillows have been dented as though a person has been resting his head on them. Pyjamas left unbuttoned and neatly folded under a pillow have been found buttoned up.

Other strange happenings have included the sudden smell of strong pipe tobacco – although no one in the family smokes – the sound of footsteps ringing out from empty rooms, the aroma of old, musty books, and the stink of rotten fish. Sometimes the family would hear the ringing of a handbell from the hallway – although there was no such bell in the house. On other occasions, a candle was found lit on the cloakroom floor.

When Matthew asked Webbe about these strange happenings, he admitted he was responsible. It was his house, he told Matthew, and he could do whatever he wanted in it.

The eeriest experience of all was when Matthew came face-to-face with

---

Kidd's return

Captain William Kidd, the British sea captain whose piracy in the Indian Ocean made him notorious, was hanged at Wapping, London, in 1701, ostensibly for killing one of his crew.

His corpse was left strung up long enough for three tides to wash over it. Days later, a shadowy figure was seen emerging from the water of the old Execution Dock. In recent years, the same figure, believed to be Kidd, has been reported at Wapping Old Stairs.

Top: Irene and Jim Hough of Dukinfield, Cheshire are convinced they had the ghost of Irene's dead husband Wilf guiding them to a win of £125 at bingo. They believe their home is haunted by Wilf and Irene keeps in touch with him through a ouija board. Since establishing contact in this way, Wilf has told Irene to start playing bingo. He even tells her where to sit when playing. Wilf is now predicting a big win on the football pools.
Left: Wilf, Irene's dead husband.

GHOSTS

Webbe in his parents' bedroom and attempted to shake hands with him. His outstretched hand went right through the hand of the ghost.

Nevertheless, Matthew managed to give him a present – a doll's wooden clog which belonged to his sister.

He held it out in friendship – and experienced an eerie feeling of timelessness. The ghost grabbed the clog and thrust it into the large pocket of his coat.

The next occurrence startled even Matthew, by now well used to the peculiar. The ghost of Webbe gradually faded away to grey and then nothing, and the doll's clog vanished with him.

Who is the ghostly Robert Webbe, and why has he haunted this house so consistently?

Matthew said, "He was a grain trader who was very proud of the house he enlarged so grandly but did not live long enough to enjoy. He wanted to take the house with him.

"I think that is why he is going round and round in a strange sort of time loop, trapped by his own will in infinity. From time to time, someone in the house provides him with enough psychic energy to allow him to make contact."

Ironically, when Matthew once got in touch with the ghost to ask him questions raised by his research into local history, Robert Webbe said he did not believe in ghosts, and that there were none in the house!

A husband's agony

Soon after chimney sweep Samuel Bull died at his tiny cottage in the Wiltshire village of Ramsbury, his widow Mary Jane fell ill. Their married daughter, her husband and five children moved in to care for her. This made the cottage too crowded for comfort, particularly as part of it was too damp to live in. It was a worry for the family – and, apparently, for the spirit of old Samuel.

Eight months after his death, in June, 1931, the children screamed when ⁓aw their grandfather climbing the stairs to his room. Mrs Bull was not ⁓ had seen the figure of her husband many times since his

⁓hs, the family saw him many times, climbing the ⁓ife's bed, often tenderly putting his hand on her ⁓ooked sad to see his loved ones living in such

⁓ity moved the family to a newer, bigger house, ⁓again.

Children from beyond the grave

When the noise becomes too loud in Edna Rugless's home, she shouts out, "Children! Please play more quietly." It always works. The two little girls who kick up such a din obey her.

Mrs Rugless has a fine understanding with the two children. Which is unusual, because the youngsters have been dead for many years.

The children love to run around upstairs in the 300-year-old farmhouse in Devon, in the west of England. Sometimes there is a creaking noise, as though someone were riding an old-fashioned rocking horse. But Mrs Rugless said, "There's nothing frightening or creepy about them. I'm very fond of children, having had four of my own. They're more than welcome.

"Their noise doesn't usually bother me. But one afternoon I heard them run out of the bedroom and start jumping around on the landing. I went into the hall and shouted up to them to stop, and they did. Of course, in their day children were taught to be obedient."

Mrs Rugless and her husband Bill, a retired engineer, discovered the ghosts when they moved to the village of Farway. The noises from the bedroom began immediately. Their pet cat and dog refused to go anywhere near the room.

Then a friend with an interest in psychic happenings visited the couple on holiday. Mrs Rugless said, "I deliberately didn't mention the noises of the children to her, but merely asked if she could feel anything unusual in the atmosphere. She told me that the spirits of two girls, aged about four or five, were active in the house and that their names began with an E and A.

The psychic visitor said she thought the girls were friends rather than sisters. One wore fine clothes, the other not so good clothes.

Mrs Rugless called in the local vicar, the Rev Frederick Gilbert, who checked parish records and found that two four-year-old girls belonging to the same family had died in the house. One was Elizabeth, who was buried in 1844; the other was Ann, whose death was in 1902.

Mr Gilbert said, "It is quite possible that these children were so happy in this house that they have been reluctant to leave. Because of the 58-year gap between the deaths it may seem odd that they should be playmates. But we have our own limited concept of time and it may mean nothing to them."

Mr Rugless said, "I was most disturbed at first, but my attitude now is that we're lucky to have such pleasant little spirits about the place."

Spirits who want to be more than good friends

Ghosts can be as spirited as the rest of us when it comes to romance, according to American ghost-hunter Stanley Wojcik. The author of several books on the supernatural, Wojcik claimed that, from his many encounters with the spirit world, he had a considerable insight into its ghostly inhabitants. Perhaps his most startling revelation was that spirits can come to the beds of the living as astral lovers.

Wojcik, from New Jersey, announced, "Spirits are just like human beings. They are the astral counterparts of their former mortal selves. Sex after death is not biological. Spirits do make love but it is an all-cellular love, a blending of their energies."

Wojcik wrote that not only do spirits make love to one another, they also haunt the beds of real people.

He said, "Women who are unattached, unmarried or divorced attract the amorous activities of male spooks for some unaccountable reason.

"I have investigated numerous cases where women told me that they had actually felt possessed by ghosts. They said that they felt all the excitement of love-making."

In 1980, at the age of 70, Wojcik claimed that he had built up a network of a dozen spirit "controls". They were, he said, spirits he had attracted during his lifetime of clairvoyance.

Stanley Wojcik's claims about the love life of spirits seem to have been reinforced by the case of the sexy ghost that drove teenager Denise Dyke and her mother out of their home. The Casanova spook kept leaping from a wardrobe and slipping into bed with the 17-year-old girl.

She managed to fend him off but her mother, Florence, became so alarmed that in 1979 she and Denise moved in with relatives while her home in Cannock, central England, was exorcised.

The ghost is in his thirties, with black, greased hair, and has been pestering the family for years. He made passes at Mrs Dyke's two other daughters when they were 17.

She said, "He used to stand by the bed, but as Denise grew older he plucked up courage. He always had an eye for the girls and it was pretty obvious what he'd got his mind on."

The local vicar, who performed the exorcism, said, "I'm convinced their story is genuine. You can sense an evil presence in the bedroom."

A lovesick ghost terrorised another English family and almost devastated their home. The ordeal began early on a summer morning for the Burden family–Charles, a 62-year-old window cleaner, wife Catherine, 56, daughter Deborah, 17, and foster son Bradley, eight.

Furniture and ornaments took on a life of their own, flying through the air and smashing against the walls. The family's labrador dog, Panda, fled howling from the house, in Bournemouth, Dorset.

Charles took a phone call at work from his terrified wife, begging him to come home. He said, "I couldn't believe it when I got there. The TV was tipped over and plates were flying around.

"The table flew around and a biscuit tin whizzed past my head and crashed in the corner. As soon as I put my foot through the door, the electric heater in the hall fell over, and when I went to phone the police, the telephone flew out of my hand."

Police watched in amazement as a kitchen dresser toppled over. A senior officer said, "I have never seen anything like it."

In desperation, they brought in Dr Fred Oliver, a 95-year-old priest, who said the Lord's Prayer before calling on the spirits to depart.

Dr Oliver said, "There has been something evil in this house that has fed on fear." Then he and the police left while the family set about restoring their home to its normally peaceful state. But it did not stay that way for long.

Three days later the poltergeist returned with increased ferocity. Mr Burden said, "This time our settee was overturned. Then the ghost tried to push over the TV again. A cabinet was then thrown at me."

When the family ran outside a heavy door leaning on a garden wall fell and narrowly missed them.

This time two mediums visited the house, and arrived at the most extraordinary explanation for the happenings. They said that the ghost of a

---

She saw her own ghost

Mary Goffe was still alive when her own ghost appeared in 1691. As she lay dying at her parents' home, Mary pleaded to be taken to see her children one last time. Her parents refused, saying the journey would be too much for her. Mary slipped into a coma, and died next day, whispering that she was at peace because she had seen her family.

Her mother thought she must have been dreaming. She was wrong.

Days later, the nurse who was caring for the children in Rochester, Kent, met Mary's mother. She revealed that at 2am on the day she died, Mary had spent 15 minutes beside the beds of her little ones, gazing silently down at them before vanishing.

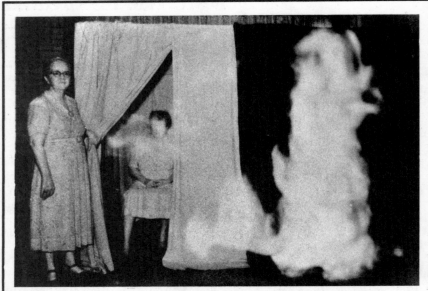

These are two from a sequence of infra-red photographs showing the whole process of a materialisation. A cloudy pillar of ectoplasm slowly builds up from the medium, Ethel Post-Parrish, to the full figure of Silver Belle, an Indian girl said to be the medium's spirit guide.

Fearsome footman

The ancient Dorset manor house at Sandford Orcas is haunted by a rapist, a tall, depraved footman who forced his attentions on serving maids in brutal fashion. Today he still revisits the scene of his conquests, usually appearing only in the presence of a virgin.

---

teenage boy called Ian had invaded the Burdens' home and had fallen in love with daughter Deborah. After she began dating boy friends, the ghost had flown into a jealous rage and attacked the house.

The mediums carried out an exorcism and advised the family to go away for a few days. When they returned, the ghost of lovesick Ian had gone.

A jealous ghost tried to part newlyweds Bob and Margaret Le Tissier, so that – in Margaret's words – "he could have me for himself".

The couple's home was a 300-year-old cottage on the site of a Cromwellian ale house at Chesham, Buckinghamshire. The Le Tissiers believed that the lovelorn ghost was the spirit of one of Oliver Cromwell's soldier's.

The first ghostly encounter came when Margaret, aged 32, and Bob, 40, were in bed. Margaret said, "I was cuddling my husband when I felt that part of the blanket soaking wet, then seconds later it was dry again. I am sure that must have been when the soldier took off his wet cape."

The couple reported other frightening incidents including eyes staring at them while they were in bed, sharp objects being pushed into their backs at night, a strange, sweet sickly smell in the hall, and horses hooves sounding in the lane outside at midnight.

Local vicar, Andrew Warburton said, "They have been through a terrible ordeal." He arranged an exorcism of the house in 1980 – and the jealous soldier retreated and was seen no more.

A sexy ghost got far too friendly for the liking of Lawrence and Brenda Massey, of Dewsbury, Yorkshire – after becoming attracted by their "emotional energy". Brenda said the chilling black figure made the couple afraid to go to bed at night.

She said, "It was like the shadowy figure of a hooded man. It was not possible to make out any features. You couldn't see its eyes, but you get a terrible sensation that the thing – whatever it was – was staring at you."

Psychic Daniel Walker's explanation was that the couple's lovemaking acted "like a magnet" to the spirit.

He said, "I have never come across anything like it before. Their emotional energy formed a medium for the spirit to appear."

Marine ghost demands justice

The restless ghost of a young American marine haunted a house in Portland, Oregon, for two years trying to convey to his mother the truth about his violent and mysterious death.

Lieutenant James Sutton had been one of a large middle-class family living in Portland at the beginning of this century. His parents, upright, respectable people, were proud when he was was accepted for training as an officer in the Marine Corps at Annapolis Military Academy.

They looked forward to his letters, which were cheerful and affectionate. When the postman arrived on the morning of October 11, 1907, his mother rushed to the letter box as usual and tore open the envelope with happy anticipation. The neatly written pages were full of good humour – but as Rosa Sutton, held, the letter, her hand began to tremble and she had the feeling that something was terribly wrong. While sitting with her family the next evening she suddenly had a sharp attack of pain, a feeling of shock. She went upstairs to read her son's letter again to make sure she had not missed anything.

The following day, still feeling troubled, she went to Mass at her local Catholic Church. Afterwards she tried to busy herself with household chores but could not shake off a strong premonition that James would come home unexpectedly. She was so sure that her daughter, Louise, was sent to prepare his bedroom.

They were taken completely by surprise when Mr Sutton suddenly arrived home from work looking distressed and very pale. "I have some bad news," he said – and told his wife gently that he had received a telegram from Annapolis informing them that their son had shot himself and was dead.

Mrs Sutton, a devout Catholic, refused to believe that her son had committed suicide. "At that instant," she wrote later, "Jimmie stood right before me and said 'Mamma, I never killed myself ... my hands are as free from blood as when I was five years old.'" No one else in the room saw or heard anything and when Mrs Sutton kept insisting he was there they merely thought the news of his death had been too much for her.

What they could not dismiss, however, were the facts that came tumbling from her lips as she listened to the unseen presence. She said her son was trying to tell them something vitally important ... he had been hit on the head with the butt of a gun ... three other men jumped on him, beat him and tried to rub his face into the ground ... they had kicked him and broken his watch. "Oh, if you could see my forehead and put your hand on my forehead, you would know what they did to me," moaned the ghost. "But I did not know I was shot until my soul went to eternity." Before disappearing, he pleaded with Mrs Sutton to clear his name and said he would never rest until it was cleared.

The phantom was persistent. On October 16 he appeared again. According to Mrs Sutton's testimony, he gave further details about his death, describing how his attackers had tried to bandage his head to hide what they had done. "My face was all beaten up and discoloured, my forehead broken and there was a lump under my left jaw."

As though to give final proof, the next time Mrs Sutton saw the ghost of her son it was with a face hideously disfigured and discoloured. Still wrapped in a great coat, he seemed to be looking for something. "It's my shoulder knot I can't find," he complained piteously.

By now the whole house was alive with the ghost's presence. The young Marine's brother, Dan, swore he had seen him on one occasion and his sister, Louise, was keenly aware of his presence. Another sister, Daisy "dreamed" one night that she had been shown a photograph of a crowd of young marines and could not take her eyes off the face of one of James's fellow officers, a man called Utley. Soon after, Mrs Sutton said her son had tried to tell her that his body had been hidden in a basement and that a lieutenant called Utley had been responsible.

First confirmation of Mrs Sutton's extraordinary experiences came three week's after James's death when Louise returned from the funeral at Annapolis bringing her brother's belongings with her. Among them was a shattered wrist watch.

The Suttons listened with mounting disbelief to the authority's official story of their son's death. According to official records Lieutenant Sutton and some friends had been to a naval dance. After it had finished they set off back to camp but were very drunk and a fight broke out. During the fracas James was thrown to the ground and heard to utter threats that he would kill the other two before morning. He returned to his tent to fetch some pistols. This

Swinging skeleton

A ghostly, weather-whitened skeleton swings from a rotting gallows on stormy nights in the Cumbrian village of Eden Hall.

They say it is the body of Thomas Nicholson, who was hanged for robbing and murdering his godfather, a butcher, in August 1767. Nicholson's corpse was left for two days on the gibbet beside Beacon Edge Road, before being buried in a shallow grave nearby.

led to his arrest and, during the attempt to seize him, he suddenly turned a gun upon himself.

Lieutenant Sutton had been buried at Arlington cemetery, but his ghost continued to haunt his old home in Portland. At first the Suttons felt there was little they could do. The naval doctors at the inquest had sworn that James's face was not disfigured. A verdict of suicide seemed in order. But after nearly two years the agonised parents made a dramatic decision. They asked for their son's body to be exhumed.

An independent inquiry revealed some staggering facts. The remains showed that he had indeed been seriously disfigured, as though he had been beaten up. His forehead was broken in and a lump formed by an injury was visible under the left side of the jaw. After the autopsy it was admitted that the angle of the bullet's entry into the body was not consistent with a self-inflicted wound. It was also found that the shoulder knot of his uniform was missing.

Soon after, the Suttons received an anonymous letter confirming the fact that Lieutenant Sutton had been murdered. The handwriting was traced and identified as that of a young serviceman who had been in the party after the naval dance. All attempts to track him down failed.

But it seemed the ghost was satisfied. As a good Catholic, he had needed to remove the stigma of suicide from his name. Mrs Sutton still caught a glimpse of him from time to time but the image grew fainter and then disappeared for good. Justice had been done.

The Black Nun's lonely search

For almost 200 years Britain's famous Guardsmen patrolled the corridors of the Bank of England in the City of London.

Their nightly vigil was to protect the gold in the Bank's vaults and started back in the 1780s at the time of the Gordon Riots in the capital.

The patrol ended in 1973 – but the Bank's other nightly visitor still makes her rounds of the Threadneedle Street buildings and gardens, searching for a lost loved one.

She's the Black Nun – so called by those who have seen her because of her thick black clothes and the dark veil which hides her face.

The apparition is supposed to be the ghost of Sarah Whitehead who roams the building looking for her brother Philip. At one time Philip worked as a clerk in the Bank but in 1811 he was arrested and charged with forgery. He

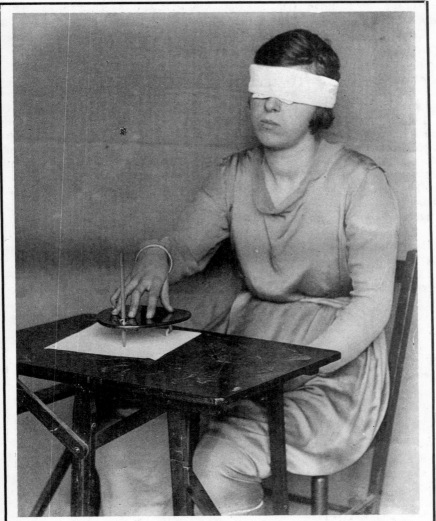

A girl using a planchette, which is a variation of a ouija board. It is used to receive communications purportedly from the dead. A pencil is attached to the board which moves on casters over a blank sheet of paper and receives messages. The operator is blind-folded to prevent conscious manipulation.

GHOSTS

was convicted and hanged – the punishment in those days for such a crime.

When Sarah didn't hear from her brother for some time she went to the Bank to look for him. The news that Philip had ended up on the gallows sent Sarah out of her mind.

The next morning she was back at the bank, dressed in mourning clothes and a thick black veil, asking if anyone had seen her brother.

For the next 25 years she would walk up and down Threadneedle Street looking for Philip, stopping passers by and going into the Bank itself.

But her lonely search didn't end with her death. Shortly after she was buried in the graveyard of the City church of St Christopher-le-Stocks, which later became part of the Bank's gardens, the lady in black was seen again.

The Black Nun, as she was then christened became a legend among the clerks who worked in the Bank at the turn of the century. Many of them claimed to have seen the desperate woman as she searched for her long-lost brother. One man claimed to have seen her in the old graveyard gardens, sobbing and pounding a stone slab with her hands.

The Guards and the gold may be long gone from the Bank, but Sarah Whitehead still keeps up her search for the brother who never came home.